Ernest Haycox

Twayne's United States Authors Series

Joseph M. Flora, Editor
University of North Carolina

TUSAS 666

ERNEST HAYCOX
Photograph courtesy of Ernest Haycox, Jr.

Ernest Haycox

Stephen L. Tanner

Brigham Young University

Twayne Publishers
An Imprint of Simon & Schuster Macmillan
New York

Prentice Hall International
London • Mexico City • New Delhi • Singapore • Sydney • Toronto

Twayne's United States Authors Series No. 666

Ernest Haycox
Stephen L. Tanner

Twayne Publishers
An Imprint of Simon & Schuster Macmillan
1633 Broadway
New York, NY 10019

Library of Congress Cataloging-in-Publication Data

Tanner, Stephen L.
    Ernest Haycox / Stephen L. Tanner.
        p. cm. — (Twayne's United States authors series ; 666)
    Includes bibliographical references and index.
    ISBN 0-8057-3898-3 (cloth)
    1. Haycox, Ernest, 1899–1950—Criticism and interpretation.
    2. Western stories—History and criticism.   3. West (U.S.)—In literature.
    I. Title.   II. Series: Twayne's Unites States authors series ; TUSAS 666.
PS3515.A9327Z85   1996
813'.52—dc20   96-19284
                                                                                    CIP

10 9 8 7 6 5 4 3 2 1 (hc)

Printed in the United States of America

For Chet and Tanner

Chapter One

Oregon Roots

Haycox and Westerns

After Ernest Haycox's death in 1950, the Western Writers of America named their annual award for the best western the "Erny." It was later renamed the "Spur," but that initial gesture of recognition and appreciation from his peers indicates the significance of Haycox's contribution to the genre. In a 1954 essay now considered a landmark in literary criticism of the western, Bernard DeVoto referred to Haycox as "the old pro of horse opera" who "came closer than anyone else to making good novels of it" and who "left his mark—I should say his brand—on the style as well as the content." DeVoto went on to claim that "others have tried to match Haycox and go beyond him, but no one as good has yet appeared."[1] This is noteworthy praise, not only because DeVoto is highly regarded as both literary critic and authority on the American West, but also because the thesis of his essay asserts that the aims of horse opera and good novels are incongruent. The compliment, in other words, is enhanced by having been given grudgingly.

Determining the scope and force of influence of a writer of popular fiction cannot be done with precision. It is unlikely that we could ever attain an accurate count of the millions of copies of Haycox novels and stories published. And it is certainly impossible ever to know the extent to which those copies have been read and circulated. Moreover, the publishing, reading, and circulating continue. A substantial amount of Haycox fiction is perpetually in print.

Although any estimate of Haycox's popularity and influence will be only approximate, the following considerations suggest that his fiction did much to shape the American public's vision of the West from the late 1920s to the 1950s. First of all, the quantity of his fiction is substantial. In a writing career spanning 28 years, he produced about a story a month and a novel a year. In *Collier's* alone his work appeared 233 times between February 1931 and February 1949, an average of 13 times a year for 18 years. Others, such as Frederick Faust (Max Brand), have been considerably more prolific but have not matched the consistent quality of Haycox's writing. Faust himself condescendingly joked about the quality of his voluminous production, calling it "brainless drip." Haycox, though he occasionally made playfully modest remarks about his magazine writing, respected what he was doing and was convinced it was worth doing well. He was temperamentally resistant to the temptations of hack work, of coasting with easy, marketable stories. His efforts to improve his craft were unflagging. Ambition and industry were hallmarks of his character.

Another consideration in estimating the impact of Haycox fiction on the American imagination is its wide dissemination in various media. Haycox stories appeared in *Collier's* and the *Saturday Evening Post* when those magazines were most popular, before the age of proliferating specialty magazines. They were found in many homes, in most barber and beauty shops, and in waiting rooms of every kind. *Collier's* reportedly increased its run by 50,000 when a Haycox story appeared. In addition to being serialized in *Collier's* and *Post*, Haycox novels were syndicated in newspapers and eventually appeared in hardcover editions from Doubleday, Doran (1929–37) and Little, Brown (1937–55). As the paperback industry emerged, Haycox novels appeared in one edition after another. Editions in braille began to appear in the late 1930s, and during World War II, Armed Services Editions of 10 Haycox titles, more than of any other living author, were distributed to men and women in military service around the world.[2] Haycox also enjoyed considerable popularity in England. As with the fiction of Raymond Chandler, the British were quicker to recognize the literary quality of Haycox's novels than was his American audience. And of course popularity in the United States and Britain was followed by translations into many languages.

Many Haycox novels and stories were adapted for movies and television. John Ford's *Stagecoach* is the most notable example. This film did much to launch John Wayne's extraordinary career. In fact, the list of actors who appeared in film versions of Haycox stories is a roll call of Hollywood stars during the 1930s and 1940s. And a number of Haycox stories found their way into television's love affair with the western in the following decades. James Stewart's first television role and Ronald Reagan's last before becoming governor of California were in adaptations of Haycox stories for "General Electric Theater."

In short, Haycox was a productive and popular author of westerns when this genre had its widest appeal in pulp, slick, and paperback fiction and on the silver screen. During the 1930s and 1940s he provided much-imitated examples of more psychologically complex heroes, more fully developed and interesting heroines, more detailed and evocative description of setting, more historically accurate events, more complicated plots, more effective style, and more challenging themes. Owen Wister and Zane Grey contributed much to the creation of the western, and Frederick Faust did much to make it popular, but Haycox had perhaps the most profound effect on how such stories were written. Since Haycox's time, Louis L'Amour has made a remarkable impact on the genre, but in a very different way. His impact results from popularity. He kept the category alive during a time when publishers were withdrawing from it. But rather than expanding and enriching the genre, his example has mainly served to narrow the range of what publishers think will sell. And, as Richard S. Wheeler has argued, L'Amour's books have turned away better-educated readers, particularly women, from reading westerns.[3] Haycox, on the other hand, as Luke Short, Frank Gruber, Wayne Overholser, Nelson Nye, D. B. Newton, Richard S. Wheeler, and other writers of westerns have frequently and generously acknowledged, provided new paradigms for others to employ. Moreover, he widened the audience for western stories by enlarging the possibilities of what a western story might be. Scholars of American popular fiction agree in recognizing his eminence.[4]

Haycox's influence on other writers of westerns indicates that his fiction had an indirect as well as a direct effect on America's conception of the West. His impact on other writers is accurately appraised in this tribute by D. B. Newton:

> Haycox very nearly succeeded, singlehanded, in doing for the standard Western what Hammett and Chandler did for the private eye detective story—made it respectable. More than any of the "big" novels like *The Big Sky* and *The Oxbow Incident*, which after all had very little to do with the kind of thing we were writing, he showed us how to take ourselves and our ordinary Westerns seriously, with a certain amount of self-respect, and not think of ourselves as nothing more than "pulp-writers" and hacks, as some people would have us do. In his short stories perhaps even more than his novels, he showed us how to find significant themes in the Western and how to develop them, without forcing ourselves out of our chosen mold of popular fiction.[5]

In addition to its quantity, quality, and wide dissemination, Haycox's fiction is notable for its scope. It provides a comprehensive portrait of the West over a considerable length of time: its regions, events, conflicts, and values. His favorite setting was his native Oregon, but he located stories in most of the western states, from Alaska to the Mexican border and from the Pacific coast to Kansas. He wrote of events occurring from the 1840s to the 1940s. Most of the important developments brought about by the opening of the West find treatment in his fiction: pioneering on the Oregon Trail, building the transcontinental railroad, gold rushes in Montana and Oregon, cattle drives, range wars, cattlemen versus sheepmen, cattlemen versus homesteaders, Custer's defeat, military campaigns against the Indians of the Southwest, land rushes, water projects, lumbering, steamboating, rodeoing, even commercial fishing in Alaska and the early years of Hollywood. And his stories are filled with the multitude of human types involved in these developments. He recognized early in his career the rich variety of people and conflicting interests in each section of the West. The setting of his story "Lin of Pistol Gap," for example, shows this awareness: "As large as some of the Eastern States, this county—named Cayuse—held within its borders every Western type. The cowpuncher and cattleman, the herder, the prospector and miner, the gambler and adventurer, the soldier and the reservation Indian rubbed shoulders. . . . These classes had almost nothing in common and their interests warred at nearly every point."[6] Haycox made a career of portraying these classes and interests.

Had he not chosen to be a fiction writer, Haycox could have been an excellent historian. He had a historian's interests and inclinations. He accumulated a fine library of historical material, which remains intact as the Haycox Memorial Library at the University of Oregon. He compiled volumes of notes on western history, preferring primary sources such as diaries, ledgers, memoirs, and frontier newspapers. He traveled often to visit and absorb the locations he wrote about. Historical accuracy and a keen curiosity about the everyday activities and the moral and social mores of a time and place distinctively mark his narratives. He was an author of stories about people in the West, not simply a writer of westerns. As Saul David perceptively observes, "The people don't simply move against a background, they illumine the background and it illumines them and the sum of it is 'western' as the sum of fish and salt water is sea. It is art, not life, of course, but the feel of real people, of a real time, is in the stories as the feel of the real sea is in the aquarium."[7]

Unlike the dime novelists and many of the pulp-western hacks, Haycox treated the West seriously and with respect, partly because he was a westerner himself, partly because of his historical temperament, and partly because his conservative disposition inclined him toward a sympathetic interest in the past. Owen Wister, who did so much to invent the western, was a dedicated conservative who thought the West might remain a repository for the old virtues. Haycox perpetuated this attitude. He genuinely admired frontier values and may have been responsible for keeping the western conservative as long as it remained so. The West symbolized for him not only a region of colorful adventure but also a realm of freedom and endeavor in which individuals, if they met its challenges, could establish satisfying relationships with their environment and one another. More than any writer of formula westerns before him, he examined the moral-cultural motives that animated the westering experience. Besides the riding and shooting in his fiction, there is significant moral and psychological struggle and discovery. In fact, many of his short stories lack the riding and shooting altogether. Instead, the action is primarily inner conflict, trials of character generated in the ordinary course of frontier life. These vivid miniatures have the cumulative effect of making the violent and melodramatic actions of the Old West myths seem merely the agitated surface of a deep, slow-moving stream. Taken as a whole, Haycox's fiction displays a greater interest in the moral and psychological character of the West than in fast-action adventure for its own sake.

Much early cowboy fiction was fantasy and the audience knew it. Haycox often wrote according to formula, but not merely according to fantasy. Readers have sensed this. It has enabled them to take the formulaic conventions with a grain of salt and at the same time embrace uncritically the realistic detail and the fundamental moral vision embodied in the action. His narratives engage readers who do not care for westerns in general. Behind the well-crafted storytelling are intimations of his personality, his sympathetic attitude toward a much misrepresented era and his affinity for the individualistic frontier code. The storytelling has a resonance lacking in most westerns because Haycox was, to a modest degree, a moral philosopher, perhaps even a political philosopher. His letters reveal explicitly the ideas and attitudes only intimated in his fiction. Those ideas and attitudes derive largely from turn-of-the-century populism: producerism rather than consumerism; a defense of endangered crafts (including the crafts of agriculture); opposition to the new class of public creditors and to the machinery of modern finance; opposition to wage labor; and fierce adherence to property ownership and the personal independence it confers. To an early twentieth-century audience suspicious of the late capitalistic system, Haycox country provided what Luke Short, in a tribute to Haycox, called "a magical nostalgia."[8]

As the frequent appearance of western stories in *Collier's*, the *Saturday Evening Post*, and other popular magazines of Haycox's era suggests, the audience for such writing was large. Robert G. Athearn points out in *The Mythic West in Twentieth-Century America* that although scholarly interest in the West was emerging in the first decades of the century, "the main thrust of the West in print was to be found in fiction and popular presentation. And it was here that Americans gained much of their impressions of the West, not from more formal writing or in the classrooms."[9] There were increasing attempts by historians to separate fact from myth, but they made little impression on the public compared with the effects of popular fiction. As an influential part of that fiction, Haycox's narratives shaped our conception of the West much the way the novels of Charles Dickens molded our images of his England or those of William Faulkner or Margaret Mitchell's *Gone with the Wind* colored our picture of the South. In some small way, Haycox's vision of the West, with its magical nostalgia, may have contributed to the large migration to the West following World War II.

Measuring Haycox's literary achievement is difficult because his writing has been lumped into a subliterary genre with vague criteria for discriminating quality among its practitioners. Moreover, the place of westerns in relation to what is often termed "serious literature" is far from clear. Locating the point at which a superior writer of popular fiction enters the realm of significant literature requires an art of triangulation not yet perfected. The cowboy novel deflects literary criticism by minding its own business and posing and answering its own questions. Its formulas, properties, and myths are so fixed and familiar that they discourage sophisticated literary analysis. As one of Haycox's reviewers put it, "Western stories are western stories and as such need little other description of characters, plot, or purpose."[10] Haycox's status as a writer, his reputation, and perhaps even the shape of his career were largely determined by the way westerns were treated by reviewers and ignored by critics. He died before serious literary criticism of the western emerged. During his time reviews were brief, condescending, and superficial, often little more than listings or occasions for wisecracks about guns that never needed reloading and chaste, pine-scented romance between taciturn cowpokes and prudish schoolmarms. If the usual put-down of westerns is accepted, Haycox is disqualified from literary merit at once.

Even the most skillful author of popular magazine fiction confronts limited possibilities for literary respect. That market demands readability and entertainment, and the cultured literary taste of our century valorizes complexity and uncertainty, often pessimism and despair. Happy endings are suspect. To complicate is the obligation of the writer who expects serious attention. A comparison of Ernest Haycox and Ernest Hemingway reveals how the sharp distinction between high-brow and low-brow fiction determines literary prestige. These authors had much in common. Both were born in 1899 and enlisted in World War I in their late teens. Both started as newspaper reporters and began publishing short stories in the early 1920s. Both chose to write about the world of weapons and violence in which physical strength and courage are admired and manifest themselves in a masculine code of grace under pressure that derives from the American frontier. The fiction of both displays a distinctive sensitivity to landscape on the part of stoic heroes who, beneath a tough exterior, harbor a melancholy sensitivity. As Philip Durham observes in an essay on Hemingway and the western code, the Hemingway hero who fights wars in Italy and Spain and shoots lions in Africa is essentially the same hero who rides the mountains and deserts of Haycox's novels.[11] Both authors were influential stylists with many imitators who discovered that their distinctive styles were difficult to reproduce. And the subject matter of both, stripped to its essence, is nostalgia. Hemingway admired Haycox's fiction. In an autobiographical communication to the *New York Herald-Tribune Book Review* in 1950, he mentioned that he was dissatisfied with current fiction but read the *Saturday Evening Post* whenever it had a serial by Haycox.[12] Gertrude Stein, who had encouraged the young Hemingway, is also reported to have admired Haycox's novels (J. Haycox 1979, x). Haycox mentioned Hemingway several times in letters to friends. He recognized Hemingway's skill, but his own orientation toward a popular audience caused him to question what he considered Hemingway's limited range of sentiments and cryptic manner of conveying them.

From the first, Haycox's writing experience was linked to the commercial market. Though admired by Hemingway and Stein, two of the most famous stylists of his age, his fiction, when measured by the highest literary standards, remains compromised by its association with magazine horse opera. But it is a remarkable achievement nevertheless. As Brian Garfield insists, "Haycox was never an ink-stained hack, never a writer-for-rent. He took both his craft and his craftsmanship seriously. He knew the slick market he worked for and he wrote toward it deliberately; but he put his very best into every line he wrote—and his best was very good indeed."[13] James Fargo also considers him more that just a writer of commercial fiction: "He was an artist of integrity, a painstaking craftsman who managed to hang onto a large part of that integrity even while making a literary living in the marts of magazine fiction."[14]

An Oregon Education

Born in Portland three months before the turn of the century, Haycox grew up in a world not far removed from the nineteenth-century frontier he spent a lifetime imaginatively re-creating. Looking back from mid-century on his formative years, he said that he "saw this part of the country change from backwoods, horse-and-buggy, jack-of-all-trades living, to the present industrialism. We were the last section, perhaps, to go through this. My boyhood was spent in logging camps, shingle mills, ranches, small towns. It was a free and easy world. Barring hard times, a man could always get a job at something—for he knew a smattering of several trades; he was an independent, footloose and optimistic man."[15] His perception of the region that shaped him is further revealed in his 1948 essay "Is There a Northwest?" Northwesterners, whom he considers to be much like westerners in general rather than a distinct regional type, are, he claims, more open and optimistic than their eastern counterparts and have a strong sense of personal autonomy and resistance to collectivism. They are middle-class, lacking in class consciousness, and politically conservative. In economics, they have been primitive operators dealing with natural resources. Not "boisterous, bawdy extroverts," they tend to avoid excess or flash and shy away from intemperate action. They produce few zealots and reformers. Having a certain stamina and straightness, they are an agricultural community that distrusts big business or private fortune. They suspect that great power is eventually destructive, and although they advocate growth, they nevertheless distrust it.[16] This characterization no doubt reveals more about the personal attitudes and values that animate Haycox's fiction than about the realities of the West. But in any case, his perceptions, whatever their accuracy, derive from the time and place in which he spent his most impressionable years.

Haycox's father, William James Haycox, once described himself as a westerner through and through. He was born in Stockton, California, in 1877, the son of an English-born paint foreman for the Southern Pacific Railroad who eventually took his family to a cooperative colony in the Nehalem Valley near Mist, Oregon. William moved around restlessly, as his father had done, and worked at many of the jobs the West of his time offered: farming, railroading, sheepherding, logging and lumbering, steamboating, and public agency work. In 1898 he married Bertha Burghardt in Portland. Raised in the Portland area, she was from a family of German origin that had moved there from Wisconsin. Their only child, Ernest James, was born 1 October the following year. William was never satisfied with his current situation and was continually on the move. This meant that Ernest's early schooling was fragmented. He may have attended as many as 12 schools before high school, which must have involved loneliness and the necessity to prove himself repeatedly in new environments. His wife described him as having been a solitary and sensitive child who never belonged to any group; hence his inclination from high school on to belong to many organizations. His parents' marriage ended in divorce before he was 11. Apparently the incompatibility of their personalities was exacerbated by William's rootless wandering. After the separation, Ernest went to live with his father's brother Frank at Mist. He spent nearly two years there associating with four cousins— three boys and a girl, Mary, who became his favorite. Mary, many years later, remembered him at that period as being good-natured, uncomplaining and courageous enough to thrash the local bully.[17]

These months were his last experience of childhood family life. He returned to Portland on the threshold of his teens and lived on his own, with only occasional contact with his parents, each of whom soon remarried. He said little about his childhood, even to close friends; yet one of those friends, a fellow writer of westerns, Robert Ormond Case, said, "No evaluation of Ernest's contribution to contemporary literature would or could be valid without reference to the effects of his . . . childhood."[18] Similarly, another friend, the editor Howard Cady, suggested that Haycox's skill in characterization owed much to his varied and challenging childhood experiences (J. Haycox 1979, vii). The bits of information available about his early years on his own suggest that he was self-reliant and resourceful, forced by necessity to learn hard truths about human nature and survival. At 11 he was selling newspapers, having to sell 10 papers in the morning before he could buy a breakfast of coffee and doughnuts. Selling papers, he recalled, "was tough. In the first place, I wasn't much of a salesman, and the rest of the boys were continually chasing me off the best corners. But I used to make enough for a 10-cent breakfast pretty regularly." From selling papers he moved on to odd jobs such as washing dishes in several Portland hotels and acting as a delivery boy. Following what he described as a "family habit to break away early from home and have a personal look-see," he went to San Francisco at 14 (Etulain 1966, 35). He worked for a while selling magazine subscriptions, then as a delivery boy in a hat factory, and finally, because he liked travel, as a news butcher selling papers and snacks on trains. He was not very good at it, and his route was not profitable: "It was from Oakland to Sacramento, California, with now and then a trip to Mount Diablo. Either run was too short. Few passengers felt the need to buy anything from the butcher. I was little more than a silly intruder in the cars." He didn't stay with the job long, but he learned such devious techniques as selling salted peanuts first to make people thirsty, tampering with Crackerjack boxes to stretch his stock, and shortchanging. He made barely enough to pay for meals and a flophouse room, and he admitted wryly that his "moral being unquestionably suffered injury."[19]

Unlike his elementary education, his high school years were spent at one school: Lincoln High School in Portland. He supported himself by miscellaneous jobs, the most steady of which was being bellhop at an apartment hotel, a job that included board and room. He was a good student, with a marked aptitude for English and history. He joined the Glee Club and Tolos, one of the school's four intramural societies. As a member of the latter he took part in debate and participated with a team that won the debate championship of the West Coast. He was attracted to writing and joined the Scribblers, a group who met to read and discuss each other's works. He served as literary editor of the Tolos, and during his senior year was on the staff of *The Cardinal*, an annual that appeared in monthly sections and served as the school's literary magazine (Etulain 1966, 39–40). His principal ranked him in the top 20 percent of his class and recommended him as a young man of "exceptional mental ability, far above the average of his age."[20]

During high school, on 1 June 1915, he joined the Oregon National Guard. Though in his sixteenth year, he passed himself off as 18. His motive, he said in an essay addressed to his classmates, was not patriotism but "a splendid chance for a vacation combined with a new and fascinating profession."[21] He got that splendid vacation the following summer when his unit was called to the Mexican border to help quell the forces of Pancho Villa. His group was ordered south on 29 June 1916. After a week's stay in San Diego, they marched south about 20 miles to Palm City in the Otay Valley. They drilled three hours in the morning and generally had the afternoon off unless they were assigned to such tasks as clerical duty or watering the mules. Their most exciting and violent engagement was raiding a watermelon patch. It was a pleasant adventure for a 16-year-old and at the same time taught him neat-ness, hygiene, precision, and the value of physical fitness.[22] It furthered the lessons of work and responsibility that life on his own had begun.

The most revealing document from his early life is the long letter he wrote to his cousin Mary while on the train from Oregon to the Mexican border.[23] With the candor and idealism of a young man approaching 17, he expressed his interests and aspirations. No one saw him off at the station, and reflecting on the way most of the soldiers had sweethearts to kiss them good-bye, he observed that having a girl brings out the best in a man: "It keeps his ideals brighter and it makes him plan and look forward into the future." One girl seemed to put all the force of her nature into a kiss. "I sure wish that I had a girl that would kiss me that way. I'd want nothing more." Because he has no such "idol to worship," he asks Mary to write and encourage him, for "I have the strange feeling that if I could be made to study I might amount to something. Doesn't that sound funny. But really I believe that I will amount to something someday." At this point he is considering a future in farming, although farming at times seems too tame. "But then the line of action that I have mapped out will keep me going. For if you must know, I don't intend to be a hayseed and never get beyond my farm. Nothing like that. I have a much wider idea." The letter speaks of duty, sacrifice, and man's abiding "elemental passions" that make violent conflict inevitable. In a postscript he says, "Mary, it's great to be a soldier of fortune and have the country passing beneath your feet. New country, new scenes, new friends, new experiences, and a new and perhaps better conception of life."

Reading this letter with a knowledge of his later career, one recognizes intimations of the ambition that energized him and the subjects that preoccupied him. The ambition was manifest in his unrelenting productivity and commitment to improving his craft. As for subject, the yearning of a lonely wandering man for a woman who could serve as the focus of his efforts and ideals, the hunger for adventure and new country, the necessity of masculine strength in a world of physical conflict—all these are the essential raw materials of his stories. A critic could charge him with arrested development, but that would be a distortion. He matured beyond the youthful romanticism, idealism, naïveté, and heroic enthusiasm of this letter; but that is not to say he rejected those attitudes entirely. He was of a time and place and temperament that tolerated them in a sympathetic though not undiscerning way.

Haycox's letter also indicates that, although he had farming in mind, he already was interested in writing. The seven-page letter is typed on a little typewriter he has brought with him. He mentions that he has his "little desk and equipment all rigged up" for the thousand-mile trip. And he has brought books with him to study. He has a sense of audience and asks Mary to imagine the landscape he describes. He writes the letter over several days and self-consciously uses a series of asterisks to indicate the passage of time. In a rudimentary way his literary inclinations are revealed in how he sees the letter as an object to be crafted. The literary aspirations suggested in this letter were confirmed by his participation with the Scribblers and his contributions to *The Cardinal* when he returned to high school. Between October 1916 and June 1917, nine of his pieces appeared in that high school publication, and a tenth appeared four months after graduation.

That graduation diverged from the usual pattern. When the United States entered World War I in the spring of 1917, Haycox and some of his classmates enlisted and were given their diplomas without taking their last examinations. The first months of his service were spent guarding tunnels and power flumes in eastern Washington and pursuing members of the International Workers of the World. Late in 1917 he went to France with an infantry unit and remained there 14 months, serving as sergeant instructor in small arms and automatic weapons and as a platoon leader. He returned from France in February 1919 and was discharged the following month. Although he reported on his college application form that fall that he was being treated for a temporary nervous condition and heart strain owing to his military service, he enjoyed his time in the army and experienced no Lost-Generation disillusionment. In 1942 he wrote to a young friend, "I hope you find the army to your liking. My own period of service in an infantry outfit was probably one of the most satisfying times of my life."[24] Instead of joining the world-weary expatriates among his contemporaries in the cafés of Paris, he worked at commercial fishing in Alaska during the summer and enrolled at Reed College in Portland in the fall. Those expressions of ambition in the letter to his cousin Mary were not boyish posturing. With no money except what he had earned himself, he took advantage of veteran benefits to help pay for his education.

He was aiming for a writing career by the time he applied to enter Reed College. Under the question regarding his academic intentions, he wrote that he wanted to study English literature and "to equip myself for fiction writing."[25] In a radio interview in 1942, he recalled that "up until I was 18, I wanted to be a farmer. . . . But I had always been troubled with the desire of self-expression, which is a very powerful motive in writing: and I had been writing odds and ends since I was a youngster of fourteen" (Etulain 1966, 45). He was encouraged in his writing by the instructor of his beginning English class, a former Rhodes scholar, who praised his descriptive skills and gave him an A$^+$ for the course. This may have clinched his intention to be a writer. It prompted him to join the staff of the college newspaper, the *Quest*, for which he wrote three playful articles about campus life (Etulain 1966, 46). He did well in his classes and joined the honor fraternity. The curriculum at Reed did not offer a wide range of courses for someone intending to be a writer, so after one year he transferred to the University of Oregon in Eugene.

At the University of Oregon he was drawn to journalism and continued, as he had done at Lincoln High School and Reed College, to grasp opportunities to contribute to school publications. He wrote a column on the campus scene for the daily *Emerald*, and in his senior year was the first editor for the newly established *Sunday Emerald*, which served as a sort of literary magazine. During his sophomore and junior years he was associated with *Lemon Punch*, the university humor magazine, and was elected to the Lemon Punch Society and later to Hammer and Coffin, the national society of humor magazines. While editorial editor in 1922, he received a letter stating that *Lemon Punch* had jumped from a ranking of twenty-seventh to fifth among college humor publications across the nation. He also edited the feature section for the *Oregana*. In addition to contributing to these campus publications, he wrote several book reviews for the Sunday issue of the Eugene *Morning Register* (Etulain 1966, 50–57).

More important to his future writing than this journalism was the stimulation toward commercial fiction writing provided by his college experience from 1920 to 1923. The University of Oregon at that time was the seedbed for a modest flowering of popular-fiction writers. A few years earlier, Edison Marshall, who achieved considerable success as a writer of romantic adventure, had helped to establish Ye Tabard Inn, a chapter of Sigma Upsilon, a national literary honorary society. This club generated considerable enthusiasm for writing, and Marshall's success at selling stories, beginning while he was still at the university, provided a model and incentive for others, including Haycox, who won the 1921 Edison Marshall Prize for the best short story by an undergraduate. One of Haycox's first national publications, written soon after receiving that prize, was a feature article on Marshall, who was just 27 at the time, titled "A Persistent Writer's Success."[26] The persistence emphasized in this piece became the guiding principle of his own writing life. Marshall, an Oregonian just four years his senior, provided Haycox with an immediate and enticing example of success. During his junior year, Haycox was president of Ye Tabard Inn, and he and other members were actively submitting their writing to magazines. According to a report in the *Emerald*, the group was honored as "leading the field in the number of active members contributing to current magazines."[27]

Haycox wrote his prize-winning story for W. F. G. Thacher's course in short-story writing. That course was the beginning of a significant and long-lasting friendship. Thacher provided him good practical instruction in magazine publishing, aided him in placing his first stories, and remained until Haycox's death his closest confidant regarding his literary aims and performance. "Most of my success in writing," he once acknowledged, "I owe to the inspiration and direction of Professor W. F. G. Thacher . . . who started me off right."[28] His letters to Thacher over the years provide a record of his deepest convictions, ambitions, and artistic soul-searching. They express his intelligence, his philosophical and political ideas, his psychological insights, and his knowledge of literary craft in ways unavailable to him in his fiction. Readers of westerns want action rather than ideas. Some of his best writing went into those letters, and they are an illuminating complement to his fiction.

After graduating from Princeton with a degree in English, Thacher had come to Portland in 1902 as an editorial assistant for a literary magazine called the *Pacific Monthly*. The magazine ceased publication in 1911, and he taught at Portland Academy and worked in advertising until taking a position in 1914 at the University of Oregon, first as a professor of English and later as a professor of journalism and advertising as well. He had been active in writing organizations at Princeton and founded Ye Tabard Inn his first year in Eugene. He wanted very much to publish and studied the magazine market intently. He told a correspondent, "I really think that I know about as much about the placement of publishable material (especially in the field of fiction) as anyone, with the possible exception of a few professionals and literary brokers."[29] He was immensely interested in pulp stories and probably knew more about them than any other college professor in the country. He once collaborated with a psychology professor to study the effects of pulp fiction on its audience. In 1936 he wrote to Robert Ormond Case, a writer of magazine fiction who was a friend and classmate of Haycox, expressing his respect for popular fiction: "Some of the very best work that has ever been done in the world of prose fiction has been simply pot-boiling; and some of the worst, the self-conscious attempt to write up to an assumed level of so-called intellectual quality."[30]

Although Thacher failed to publish very much of his own writing, his students benefited from his expert knowledge of the professional and commercial side of story writing. Part of his teaching method was to have the student study the market: "He is expected to learn all that he can about the magazine—its background; its editorial policies; its contents; its business and advertising practices; its physical make-up; and so on." In this way the student is forced to compare his stories with the writing that expert and hard-boiled editors are actually printing. This can be disillusioning, says Thacher, but disillusionment is necessary. "I have little use for writing *in vacuo*. A story is written to be read, and it is well for the student to find out as early as possible just what kinds of stories *are* read."[31] He advised a young writer in a letter that almost anyone can succeed as a professional writer if he pays the price in effort: "If one wants to write and publish, he has to write for the market, learn the kind of stuff the editors are using, and determine for himself what variety of the current story he himself can produce."[32]

Haycox was introduced to this pragmatic and commercial approach to the fiction business in his first story-writing class. He embraced it and learned it well. It guided him until the 1940s, when a growing desire to write serious novels led him away from the magazine audience. But by then the habits so successful in writing for *Collier's* and the *Saturday Evening Post* were ingrained and difficult to modify. He struggled during his final years to change those habits and redirect his creative energies, but death from cancer prevented him from completing the transition.

With energy and persistence Haycox began writing and submitting stories during his first year at the University of Oregon. Thacher's course gave impetus and direction to an ambition generated in high school. From this point on his career was characterized by industry and determination. During the summer of 1922, instead of his usual itinerant work, he chose to devote himself to writing. Living in an old chicken coop behind his fraternity house on a steady diet of beans, he gave his full attention to producing stories, eventually papering three walls of his tight quarters with rejection letters. He had begun submitting stories early in 1921, and the *Overland Monthly* published two of them by the end of that year. He received no money for these, but at this point being published was worth as much as money to him. *Sea Stories*, one of the Street and Smith Corporation pulp magazines, was the first to pay him for a story. It was a story that had been turned down 14 times by other magazines. Obviously, he wasn't easily discouraged. Haycox later recollected, "I got $30 for that story. It was all it was worth in money, but it was a victory worth far more to me. I knew what I wanted to do—what I had to do, and set about doing it. Of course I worked at many other things in between, but they were merely ways of eating until I found my pace."[33] The instruction of Thacher and the example of Edison Marshall had convinced him that persistence was everything. As a graduation souvenir, Haycox gave Thacher a bound volume of about 40 rejection slips. They came from magazines as diverse as the *Atlantic Monthly* and the *Black Cat*. The playful introduction to this little volume reflects his ambition and determination. "Let the collection grow," he says. "Let it be the proud boast of Oregon writers that they have actual, bona fide, written rejections from every magazine in America." Then when they succeed they can brag about their early disappointments.[34] Albert Richard Wetjen, one of Haycox's generation of Oregon writers, who was jealous during the 1930s of Haycox's success and particularly of his rigorous work habits, recalled a little sourly that even when Haycox was a student at the University of Oregon and had sold only a few stories, he seemed confident that he could succeed as a writer.[35]

In Haycox's article on Marshall's persistence he had said, "Quite the best thing about Eddie Marshall is that he has no false standards about 'art.'"[36] From the beginning Haycox viewed fiction writing as a practical matter of making a living. Notice the tone of this 1922 letter to a fellow writing student: "Clearing up the correspondence so's to get at the meaty matter involved in putting out saleable, malleable, and profitable fiction. Sold another to sea stories t'other day. But damn 'em, they won't publish the gosh darned stories. I figure that when they proof read them the effect is so awful they decide to junk the MSS. If I were an editor I would. They don't know how I wrote those stories."[37] The self-depreciating nonchalance here is partly a youthful pose, for he took his craft seriously and always gave it his best effort, but he had no pretensions about artistic seriousness. He complained in a letter to a friend of what he considered esthetically pretentious stories appearing in the *Dial*. They reminded him of someone "slovenly" in literary skill "who has a piece of an idea and is unable to do it up in a neat, legitimate, clean-cut package, and hides his ability and his punk piece of work under the vast blanket of 'impressionism.'"[38] The mention of packaging indicates his orientation toward producing a marketable product. In the same letter, written a few months before graduation, he says, "Yes, it is nice to get a novelette across; but after all the labor I put into it, the $300 doesn't seem to be much of a windfall. Must get more next time. Can't afford to work for a cent much longer."

By the time he graduated with a degree in journalism in June 1923, Haycox had succeeded in entering the pulp magazine market. He had moved beyond the pleasant novelty of first acceptances to practical concerns of how to place more stories more profitably. Besides the first two stories in the *Overland Monthly*, not a paying pulp magazine, five stories had appeared in *Sea Stories* and one each in *Top-Notch* and *Ace-High*. One of this first group of nine stories was based on his experience on the Mexican border, and six were sea stories set on the Alaskan coast, where he had worked at commercial fishing. They clearly bear the stamp of Jack London, whose work he had admired since high school. One of those in the *Overland Monthly*, a publication once edited by Bret Harte, tells of three town officials' humane treatment of the local prostitute and has a sentimental Harte flavor. The *Ace-High* story narrates the adventure of a government agent's capture of a gang smuggling Chinese coolies across the Canadian border. None of these tales is a formula western. Looking back about a decade later, Haycox in a letter to Thacher issued the following judgment on this apprentice work: "The first three years' work I'm not professionally proud of. Those stories were pretty bad—naturally. Looking at them carefully, I have come to conclude that I always possessed a high sense of word values and a feel for color and action, but that I wasn't at all a natural story teller. The early stories show me rather clearly that I wrote almost nothing that was a native yarn. They were all painfully synthetic."[39]

For a young man who had been left to his own devices at an early age, these college years provided direction, confidence, friendships, and a sense of belonging. He maintained strong ties with the University of Oregon throughout his life. As a student journalist, he had written of the need for a student union building. Near the end of his life he served two terms as president of the alumni association and headed the fund drive for the existing union building. Some of the friendships he made with students and faculty while at the university continued to be active and important to him for years to follow. "I came into the university," he wrote Thacher, "feeling distinctly inferior, of humble people. I can find nowhere in my family anybody who ever got by the eighth grade. I came out of the university with an inadequate education, which was my fault, but certainly without any feeling of inferiority; much more tolerant and skeptical."[40]

Chapter Two

Apprenticeship in the Pulps

Getting Started

Haycox began submitting stories to magazines as a college student in 1921. His first story in *Collier's*, one of the major glossy magazines or slicks, appeared in February 1931. In the intervening decade, he served a sort of apprenticeship in the pulp magazines. This was largely according to plan, or at least to expectation. He aimed for the top magazines from the beginning, but he knew he must pass through a period of learning his craft and was not discouraged by rejections from highly regarded magazines. In his 1922 article in the *Writer* (a periodical subtitled "A Monthly Magazine to Interest and Help All Literary Workers"), he had recommended the principle "that if you start at the bottom and work like the devil, you will some day, be 'up amongst 'em.'"[1] His belief in this principle rested largely on Edison Marshall's example and Thacher's instruction, but he was deeply committed to it. He explained to his friend Arthur Larson in 1925 that he saw two ways to succeed in writing for magazines. One was to write away without submitting anything until you were good enough to break in at the top. The other—his chosen way—was "starting with the half centers (half cent per word) and writing on up through the pulp field to the big fellows. . . . Most of us prefer serving our apprenticeship with a little pay coming in." Some pulp writers claimed they rapidly scribbled stories that catered to popular taste just for the money. Haycox was not of this sort. He viewed the pulp market as something to be exploited, and he proposed to profit from it as much as possible, but his impelling ambition to master the writing craft entailed an integrity toward his work. As he told Larson, "A man must write what he likes to write and the minute he goes in for something his heart can't accept, then he's bound to make a bobble of it."[2] He wrote to another close friend in 1930, "As you know, I have no sympathy at all for the guy who kids himself into thinking that art can be prostituted. A man does what he does, that's all. . . . On the other hand, I can't stir up much enthusiasm for the fellow who considers every word he turns out to be anointed with holy unguents."[3] In looking back on the stories of his apprentice years from the point of his highest achievement, when he might have dismissed them as beginning hack work, he said, "I don't hold to the notion that a writer can ever do casual work; he necessarily operates at the top of his capacity at any given time or he's not valid; therefore these stories represent the best I could write at the time I wrote them."[4]

Before he turned to writing fiction full time, Haycox put his training in journalism to work after graduation by taking a job with the Portland *Oregonian*. He began with the usual assignments of writing obituaries and reporting minor local happenings. He performed well enough to be offered a night editorship but declined because he wanted to do his own experiencing and writing. Instead, he was promoted to the night police beat. That must have seemed to a young reporter an opportunity for exciting experiences and writing, but he soon found himself grinding out routine reports of the perennial holdups, burglaries, suicides, and traffic accidents of a growing city. And any attempts at literary touches were summarily squelched at the copy desk. But the most disappointing aspect of newspaper work for an aspiring creative writer was the time required. The usual night beat ran from 6:00 P.M. to 2:30 A.M. To produce his fiction, Haycox often returned from his shift at the police station to the *Oregonian* building, hiked eight floors to the editorial room, and worked through the wee hours. He kept manuscripts circulating and continued his habit of defiantly pinning rejection slips on the wall. After a few months of this persistence, he was making as much from his fiction as from his meager cub reporter's salary (Etulain 1966, 71–73).

After eight months of newspaper work, he gave it up in April 1924. Success in placing his stories had given him confidence to attempt the risky step of earning a living exclusively by writing fiction. "I never was a good newspaperman," he later admitted. "I couldn't get at the fundamentals. They interfered with my love of creating stories."[5] That love must have been intense during his first year out of college, for during 1924 he published 17 stories in *Western Story, Detective Story,* and *Sport Story*. With this taste of success, he decided he should go to New York City to be close to the headquarters of the magazine business. He had saved enough money to buy an automobile and make the long drive from coast to coast, but not enough to sustain him for long when he arrived. He rented a small apartment near Greenwich Village and began what he called his "starving" period.

The manuscripts he brought with him and those he wrote there were designed for the *Saturday Evening Post*, the primary target of his ambition at the time. But he failed in that objective, and in fact placed nothing in the *Post* until 1943. His meager funds depleted, he consulted with Frank E. Blackwell, editor-in-chief at Street and Smith, who had bought some of his stories for *Western Story*. This man, Haycox reported to Thacher, "was more like an elderly Scotch Presbyterian deacon than the flamboyant personality one might imagine as befitting the role of top hand of his particular bunch of supposedly cow-poke writers." Haycox explained his aspirations and problems while Blackwell listened sympathetically. At the conclusion of the interview, the editor, according to Thacher's account, said, "Young man, I have just one piece of advice for you. Learn how to write a western. Once you have mastered that, the rest is up to you."[6] It is hard to imagine better advice for that young writer at that particular time. He was a westerner with interests and aptitudes suited to the western genre, and an extraordinary market for such fiction was emerging. He had tried his hand at sea, detective, and sports stories, and even those he had already sold to *Western Story* were not westerns in the usual sense but simply stories set in Oregon. With this advice to reflect on, he returned to Oregon to recuperate from his first rather discouraging and physically draining encounter with New York City.

He soon had his objectives refocused and his determination renewed. He returned to New York in the fall of 1924, this time by rail. Aboard the same train was Jill Marie Chord, a young woman from Baker, Oregon, on her way to art school. They married the following March, after a courtship conducted on a shoestring. Jill remembers: "We used to meet three or four times a week at Central Park. I lived nearby. Sometimes when Erny had sold a short story to *Western Story Magazine* we had a rowboat ride. If he sold a novelette we had a hansom cab ride. Mostly we walked. Once, he walked me across the Brooklyn Bridge and back" (J. Haycox 1979, viii). He did a lot of walking in those days. He wrote to Arthur Larson that he walked eight miles every morning around Prospect Park and wrote 5,000 words every day, about five days a week (Larson).

He had no fondness for New York City. His long walks in the park were probably a way of allowing his imagination to return to Oregon, and it was not long before he made that return. By January 1926 he had decided that he didn't have to live in New York City to be a writer. Perhaps that was the principal thing he learned there. He longed for the western landscape and way of living. He had bought a second-hand Cadillac touring car in December. In June he and Jill loaded it with camping gear, food, and an Airedale pup, and after breakfast at Child's

serials a year.[10] The appetite for western stories was vast and for a considerable time insatiable.

Most pulp western stories were like cheap sweets: mass-produced for the undiscriminating palate, flavored for intensity rather than nuance, high in calories but low in nourishment. They were often written by people who knew little about the West and were disinclined to dispel that ignorance by research. One reading of Walter Prescott Webb's *The Great Plains* could provide a clever one of these Manhattan cowboys, as they were sometimes called, with the background material for a hundred stories. Historical authenticity and geographical accuracy seemed to matter little to most editors and readers. Many of these writers knew much more about their audience, their market, than they did about the people who constituted the characters in their fiction. Consequently, the errors and misconceptions about the West proliferated along with the popularity of the genre. Action was the lifeblood of this fiction. Character delineation was brief, often little more than descriptive tags—*redhead, lantern-jawed, dead eyes, scar-faced*—to prevent the rapid reader from getting characters mixed up. Editors discouraged self-reflection or philosophic digression. Character motivation had to be simple and unambiguous, leading to a happy sense of closure. Among Haycox's early rejection slips is this response from an editor: "This story is exceedingly well written, but it is not a story of success, and we make it a rule to print no stories of failure, or any stories that are in any way depressing."[11] The mass audience desired entertainment and escape, surface confirmation of the myths they cherished rather than unsettling analysis of them.

According to Dinan, the only rejection Frederick Faust got from a publisher of western fiction was for developing characters too fully. Frank Blackwell of *Western Story* returned three stories with the comment that there was too much character development. Blackwell understood his readers' preference for action and had simplified the pulp western plot to two types: pursuit and capture and delayed revelation, and he believed further that the latter was a minor variation of the former (Dinan, 51). Haycox's friend and fellow pulp writer Robert Ormond Case tells this story of Blackwell's concern for simple plots. Blackwell called Haycox into his office after he had bought a few of his stories: "'Haycox,' he said, 'I've bought three of your short stories, and I think we're running into plot trouble.' (Hitching his chair closer.) 'In your first story, Haycox, you had two men and one woman. In your second there were two women and one man. In your third you have one man and one woman. My God, Haycox—(whispering)—*where do we go from here?*'" (Case, 4).

Restaurant they embarked on more than a month of the unpredictable adventure afforded by automobile touring in the 1920s. Haycox wanted a good look at the West, from Arizona to Yellowstone, and apparently got it. Following this expedition, the couple, after a brief stay in Silverton, settled in Portland, where, aside from two months in Hollywood and brief trips to the East Coast, Hawaii, Greece, and locations in the West that were settings for his novels, they remained. He leased an office downtown and, dressed like a businessman, went there each weekday from nine to five to do his writing, living the life of a Republican, Rotarian, and Methodist outwardly while creating a world of romantic western adventure—Haycox Country—in his imagination.

The World of Pulp Westerns

Haycox was well advised to specialize in westerns, which in pulp magazine form were beginning their golden age early in the 1920s. That age lasted until about 1940. Speaking of this 25-year period during which the pulp western flourished, John A. Dinan says in *The Pulp Western* that "there has been, perhaps, no greater amount of written material produced in such a short time on a given theme, before or since."[7] Action fiction in general was very popular following World War I. A 1927 study in *Publishers Weekly* ranks the 54 most popular authors in America from 1919 to 1926. Zane Grey is first on that list and F. Scott Fitzgerald last. Five of the top seven are writers of action fiction.[8] According to Cynthia S. Hamilton, about two dozen pulps were being published at the close of World War I, but by the mid-1930s more than 200 pulp magazines reached 25 million readers, issuing 200 million words a year at the height of their popularity.[9] Among the pulp magazines that flourished during this period, those devoted to western stories were by far the most numerous and popular. Dinan lists 184 magazines devoted primarily to the western theme and allows that his list might not be exhaustive (Dinan, 5). *Western Story* was the most notable of these. Begun in 1919 as a replacement for *Buffalo Bill Stories* and *New Buffalo Bill Weekly*, it lasted some 30 years and was one of Street and Smith's most profitable ventures. Its circulation was approaching the half million mark by 1921 when the work of Frederick Faust (Max Brand) began to appear in it so prolifically. Haycox published 27 stories in this magazine between March 1924 and December 1927, riding the wave of its popularity. At its peak it needed six stories per issue or about 300 a year, plus a complete novel of around 30,000 words, plus four six-part

ing the wounded bird. All of Dave's bitterness about his life in this harsh environment is focused in a hate for Billy. During the night he clubs his partner with a piece of firewood, throws him into the river, and, leaving the cabin open, returns to the settlement with a false story. Entering the cabin in the spring, uneasy in conscience, he loses a grip on his sanity when he hears a scraping sound and the bird flies against his face. In hysterical flight Dave plunges into the river.

As previously mentioned, Haycox was advised by a pulp editor in 1923 to write westerns.[16] That editor probably had in mind a wider range of action stories set in the West than would come to our minds 70 years later. From the 1930s to the 1950s, the western narrowed and solidified as a genre, and Haycox played an important role in that process. But he did not immediately begin writing about cowboys and walkdowns in response to that advice. He simply followed his inclination to write stories set in Oregon. For example, between March 1924 and October 1926 he published six stories in *Detective Story*, one of the Street and Smith pulps. This magazine title immediately suggests to us the urban private eye or hard-boiled dick made so familiar by Dashiell Hammett, Raymond Chandler, and others beginning in the 1930s. Haycox's stories are nothing of that sort. They are stories of rural Oregon that happen to involve crime and detection, the detection accomplished by a rather unexceptional local sheriff—a farm community sheriff, not a cattle town sheriff. Aside from the slight emphasis on crime solving, they are indistinguishable from the stories he was placing in *Western Story* about the same time. In fact, "Too Much Spunk" (28 June 1924), one of the *Western Story* group, is the same kind of story with the same Sheriff Sanders. Three other of his *Western Story* contributions are set in the present and treat forest fires and a timber swindle.

The Burnt Creek Stories

The transition in Haycox's early stories from the subject of Oregon homesteading and farming to the subject of lawmen and outlaws is displayed in a cluster of 10 *Western Story* pieces set in the sandy hill country of central Oregon. The main character in most of these Burnt Creek stories is Dave Budd, affectionately known as old man Budd. Plump, nearing fifty, owner of a general store during the 1920s, Budd is a most unlikely hero for a pulp western magazine. He loves the land and the people and is trusting and generous. A grateful homesteader had labeled him the "shepherd of southern Deshutes County." He acutely and sym-

behind him "definitely and forever the lowlands of the restless spirit." The plot is thin and the message floridly expressed. But while the story lacks intrinsic value, it reveals several things about Haycox's start in the pulp western magazines. First of all, it shows that *Western Story* included many kinds of stories, often ones without cowboys. It reveals also that Haycox began with an interest in writing about Oregon rather than about a mythic West and with a desire to express themes and not simply narrate action adventure. He eventually turned to the usual cowboy formulas and in fact did much to shape them, but he began his career with the desire to express thoughtfully the Oregon experience. Late in his life he returned to the same pursuit with stories in *Collier's* and the *Saturday Evening Post* and his last four novels.

His early stories are really more strongly influenced by Jack London than by Owen Wister or other writers of westerns. At the time of London's death, Haycox had published in his high school annual a tribute pointing out what can be learned from London's example. He focuses on three things: "the value of personal contact, of first hand information, the greatness of the cosmopolitan view, the broadened mind, and the accomplishments and rewards that are the fighter's share."[15] In a remarkable way, these three principles, recognized at age 17, remained constants in his approach to writing. He made it a point to visit the locations he wrote about and favored primary sources in his research; he abhorred narrow-mindedness and took it to task in his stories; and the primary theme in all his fiction is the fundamental necessity of the will to fight.

The flavor of London is obvious in the five stories of fish pirates and rum runners off the coast of Alaska that he published in *Sea Stories* in 1922–23. The dominating captains and multinational sailors are near relatives of Wolf Larson and his crew in *The Sea-Wolf*. His story titled "Wolf" in *Western Story* (15 September 1924) tells of a dog that responds to the call of instinct and becomes for a while the leader of a wolf pack. This is merely a miniature and inferior version of *Call of the Wild*. At least two other contributions to *Western Story* clearly bear the London stamp: "Vengeance in the Wilderness" (6 September 1924) and "The Snowbird" (11 October 1924). These stories of Oregon trappers have the elements of male conflict in a primitive environment and the ironic touch found in London's tales of the Yukon. In "The Snowbird," for example, Billy, a blond and cheerful young giant, breaks trail in a snowstorm for his sullen partner, Dave, who resents his cheerfulness. When they arrive at their cabin, a snowbird is blown inside. Billy prevents Dave from crush-

Generalizations about narrow focus, rigid formulas, and misconceptions about the West also need qualification. *Western Story*, for example, was not simply a magazine of formula shoot-out stories. It included a considerable variety of stories with western settings. Interspersed among the stories were short information pieces on western history, geography, wildlife, and culture. There were also regular departments on the practical aspects of mining, on traveling in the West, and on other characteristics of the region. As western pulps multiplied, the standards and guidelines of *Western Story* were compromised and made more rigid in the lower-grade pulps.

It is necessary to recognize the exceptions to the usual portrait of pulp westerns in order to understand Haycox's apprenticeship during the 1920s. Unlike most pulp writers, he had a university degree and academic training in writing. Some pulp writers wrote under more than one name. Haycox used only his real name and always believed he could make something of his marketplace writing. He never resorted to masks, bullwhips, knife throwing, quick-draw gimmicks, modified weapons, mountain lion companions, or other such farfetched properties of low-grade westerns. The fact is that he had published 20 of his 27 stories in *Western Story* before he even treated the usual cowboy and shoot-out. In the mid-1920s this magazine was establishing itself, and its product was evolving. Haycox, as a frequent contributor, was likewise experimenting with a variety of stories set in the West.

His first contribution to *Western Story*, "His Ranch Lure" (1 March 1924), tells of a young Portland newspaperman who loses his way wandering in the flatlands near the Cascades. He stays with a farm couple and their pretty daughter, experiences the wholesome peace of rural life, and decides to stay. The story is set in the present and has the autobiographical elements of Haycox's newspaper work and early love of farming. The pastoral theme is explicit and romantic. Near the story's end, the young man watches a hawk at dusk and inhales "the deep rich fragrance of grasses and flowers and ripening fruits" and the scent of honey from nearby hives. He contrasts these smells with the odor of the newspaper he is holding, which reminds him of the hectic, noisy newspaper office. The sound of a bell from the barn seems "a witness of some deep and all-pervading power; carrying him away from the speculation and earthy uneasiness by the magic and mystery of its origin; lifting him by the feeling, powerful, inspiriting, that he was, for this space, standing face to face with the intangible reservoir of life, of the fountain and source of his own being." He feels kinship with the hawk and puts

Editors aimed for what would sell and insisted that writers conform to marketable formulas. "Of course if you go after the mechanics of Western stories as such," Frederick Faust noted, "you'll find that it's a simple group of rules by which one may cut the pattern of any number of yarns. And your bank account need never fail if you follow the rules, and slip carefully along the marked lines. And not so carefully at that."[12] The ravenous market and easy formulas caused many pulp western writers to feel condescending and cynical toward their craft and audience. Faust, for example, referred to his fiction as "brainless drip" and his audience as "child-minded people."[13] Another writer for the pulps, Allan R. Bosworth, remarks in reflecting on their heyday, "Perhaps, if we had taken our craft more seriously—if we had written each story with care and the best of our skills, and without tongue in cheek—the pulps would have endured. But in the early 1930s there was no sign of impending crash. The newsstands were rife with pulps."[14]

At their worst, pulp western magazines were like comic books without the pictures. Their colorful action covers and occasional illustrations suggest the similarity. Their town-taming heroes often had the disguises, idiosyncratic weapons, and peculiar but loyal companions (human and animal) characteristic of comic-book heroes. The action took place in a western never-never land and was as implausible as the plots were predictable.

Haycox and the Pulps

The preceding generalizations about pulp westerns are of course not entirely accurate. Many fine writers got their start and began to reveal the quality of their talent in the pulps. Some excellent stories appeared in these popular magazines, fiction rivaling the best that appeared in the slicks. Writing successfully for a mass audience and making physical action simple and exciting is, at its best, a highly specialized craft. "Serious" writers who condescendingly tried the medium in the hope of earning easy money seldom succeeded. Elmer Kelton, who is currently writing highly regarded westerns, said, "The more I studied the pulps, the greater my appreciation of the better class of stories in them. Until I approached them with an analytical mind and began trying to figure just what made them tick—with of course the intention of using that knowledge for my own benefit—I never truly appreciated the craftsmanship and sometimes outright genius which went into them." He mentions Haycox in particular as a pulp writer who "moved on up to a high plane of literature" (Dinan, 86).

Contents

Preface

Ernest Haycox was a prolific writer. To describe and comment on his fiction more than briefly would require an inordinate amount of space and involve considerable repetition. I have chosen instead to limit my treatment of individual novels and stories in order to focus on the shape of his career. The story of that career is interesting in itself, involving as it does determined effort, growth, and achievement and incessant, thoughtfully articulated aspiration. The story is also interesting for what it reveals about the thriving industry of popular magazine fiction in America between 1920 and 1950. Haycox was a standard-setter in both pulp and glossy magazines. And the story is interesting for the way it brings into sharp focus questions about the differences—real or assumed—between "popular" and "serious" literature. Specifically, it raises the issue of how a first-rate author in an allegedly second-rate genre is to be evaluated. As a guide for my approach, I have had in mind a statement by Paul Horgan: "The best literary critic is the one who understands what the author was unable, for one or another reason, to write; and, understanding this, is able the more appreciatively to evaluate what the author was able to achieve."[1]

I have diverged from convention by not citing page numbers for quotations from Haycox's fiction. Hardcover editions are very difficult to locate, and paperback editions are so numerous and haphazardly available that little purpose is served by arbitrarily singling out one of them for citation. Moreover, I have used quotations for simple illustration rather than as vital evidence for argued interpretations, which further lessens the need for specific citation.

Because I am interested in Haycox primarily as a literary artist, I have not treated the film versions of his stories. Such treatment, particularly of the acclaimed film *Stagecoach*, is available elsewhere in the growing literature of film.

I have drawn generously from unpublished letters because they document so well the aims and stages of Haycox's development and reveal dimensions of his thought and personality not conveyed in his fiction. I am grateful to the University of Oregon Library, the Oregon State Library, the Oregon State Historical Library, the New York Public Library, and Little, Brown publishers for permission to examine and to make use of Haycox material. I am especially grateful to Ernest Haycox, Jr., for his cooperation and permission to use material from the Haycox family papers. Richard Etulain and Jon Tuska were also generous in providing information. Research time and money were provided by the College of Humanities and the Charles Redd Center for Western Studies at Brigham Young University.

Chronology

1899	Ernest James Haycox born 1 October in Portland, Oregon.
1913	Enters Lincoln High School in Portland.
1914	Works on train as news butcher during summer.
1915	Enlists in Oregon National Guard, 1 June.
1916	Spends summer on Mexican border with National Guard.
1917	Receives diploma from Portland's Lincoln High School.
1917–1919	Serves in France with the 162d Infantry.
1919	Works as commercial fisherman in Alaska and enrolls at Reed College in Portland.
1920	Enrolls at the University of Oregon.
1921	Wins Edison Marshall Prize for outstanding story by an undergraduate. First two published stories appear in *Overland Monthly.*
1922	Receives first payment for his fiction from *Sea Stories.*
1923–1924	Graduates in June from the University of Oregon with a degree in journalism. Works as reporter for *Oregonian* for nine months.
1924	Goes to New York City and begins full-time magazine writing.
1925	Marries Jill Marie Chord in New York City, 4 March.
1926	Returns from New York City to Oregon by long auto-camping trip.
1929	*Free Grass.*
1930	*Chaffee of Roaring Horse.*
1931	Writing first appears in *Collier's; Whispering Range.*
1934	*Riders West* and *Rough Air.*
1935	*Starlight Rider* and *The Silver Desert.*
1936	*Trail Smoke.*

1937   *Trouble Shooter* and *Deep West*.

1938   *Sundown Jim* and *Man in the Saddle*.

1939   Spends four months in Hollywood working for Samuel Goldwyn studios; *The Border Trumpet*.

1939–1940   Builds large house in hills above Portland; *Saddle and Ride*.

1940   Begins three-year term as director of Portland Rose Festival Association.

1941   *Introduction to Oregon* (Chamber of Commerce booklet promoting Portland); *Trail Town*.

1942   *Alder Gulch*.

1943   Writing first appears in *Saturday Evening Post; Action by Night* and *The Wild Bunch*.

1944   *Bugles in the Afternoon*.

1945   *Canyon Passage*.

1946   Begins term as president of University of Oregon Alumni Association. World premiere of the film *Canyon Passage* in Portland. Receives honorary degree from Lewis and Clark College. Works in Portland on two Hollywood films; *Long Storm*.

1947   Visits Greece as representative for the United States Mission for Aid to Greece. Elected to board of directors of Portland Chamber of Commerce.

1949   Is president of Portland Rotary Club.

1950   Has cancerous tumor removed 17 May. Dies 14 October in Portland.

1952   *The Earthbreakers*.

1955   *The Adventurers*.

pathetically observes people around him and often uses tricks to bring young lovers together, to aid the needy without damaging their pride, or to give an avaricious skinflint his comeuppance. He is willing to give others a break, even if doing so requires bending the rules. The stories have the colorful vernacular dialogue and amusing deceit in the cause of right that is characteristic of the frontier humor that reached its apex with Mark Twain. They reflect the values of western populism: "There was no crime equal to that of dispossessing a man of his land, even when a mortgage fell due. They must all work together in this country; there could be no strict accountability in seasons when the bottom fell away from the market and the desert sun burned men's hopes to a blackened shred."[17] The stories celebrate work, courage, honesty, trust, neighborly solidarity, generosity—the best of the qualities involved in settling the West. Haycox began and ended his career asserting such pioneer values in the context of Oregon's settlement, and these values undergird the large body of formula westerns that made him famous.

"Budd Dabbles in Homesteads" (1 November 1924) can serve to illustrate the Burnt Creek stories. The greedy speculator Aaron Bixby has foreclosed on Sim and Ethel Meeker. They will lose their place after 10 years of hard work. This disturbs Dave Budd, who believes in the homesteaders and is confident the land will eventually be productive. He saves the Meekers' place through an ironically suitable trick, a ruse that entraps Bixby in his own greed. Budd hires a couple of young men to pose as surveyors laying out the lines for a railroad. They don't claim to be working for the railroad, but Bixby, eager to make money by selling right-of-way property, makes the assumption and trades land with Budd, even adding some cash to the deal.

In the later Burnt Creek stories Budd appears only incidentally, and in the last of the 10, "No Gent to Fool With" (11 September 1926), he is unmentioned. Correspondingly, the focus of the stories shifts from interpersonal relations, neighborly intervention, and populist values to the sheriffs, outlaws, and chases of conventional westerns. The time is still the 1920s, but the action is straight out of the Old West. Haycox is clearly moving toward the popular formula. Burnt Creek is not mentioned; the town is Rawhide. The only continuity with the earlier stories is the fact that the hero, Lee Brent, appeared in "The Bird in the Bush" (3 July 1926), the last to mention Burnt Creek and Budd. Between these two stories, Haycox had published "Rimrock and Rattlesnakes" (10 July 1926), his first contributions to *Western Story* that really conformed to the cowboy formula. In "No Gent to Fool With," Brent, a skinny, unprepossessing redhead, is a young marshall in charge while the sheriff is away having an operation. Three bank robbers drift into town posing as homesteaders. Brent is suspicious of them and watches as they enter the bank after hours. He breaks up the holdup and shoots one of the thieves. The other two escape, leaving the banker dead. Brent pursues and is trapped by the crooks on a cliff over a bend in the river. He escapes the trap by lowering himself with a rope and dropping into the river. He comes up behind the two and tells them to give up, but they go for their guns. Brent shoots one and captures the other. This is the typical robbing, riding, and revolver wielding of the category westerns to which Haycox devoted himself in the years to follow.

Pioneers and Patriots

In the late 1920s Haycox began to turn exclusively to horse opera. That was the most profitable market for him, and he obviously found the genre congenial to his interests and talents. But in turning to cowboys, he was turning away from his keen interest in American history and particularly the pioneer experience in Oregon. This interest, however, was abiding and reasserted itself in the late 1930s and 1940s in his historical westerns and his homesteading and pioneer stories. His career was a circle, beginning with an exploration of early American history and of the pioneer era of his own region, then moving through the realm of romantic cowboy adventure, and returning to history, this time of the West and primarily of Oregon.

The Burnt Creek stories, essentially concerned with early-twentieth-century homesteading, reflect his interest in the moral and social codes and values he thought characterized the settlement of the West. In four other stories published in 1925 and 1926 he went further back in time to portray similar codes and values, back to the beginnings of Oregon's settlement in the 1840s: "The Valley of the Rogue," "Frontier Blood," "Sons of the Forest Edge," and "Light of the West." The first three are about pioneer-Indian conflicts. "Sons of the Forest Edge" clearly adumbrates the fine stories of pioneer women he would write in the late 1940s. "Light of the West" is transparent boosterism for the simple, rugged, wholesome life of the pioneer. As the title suggests, the West is presented as a guiding light for the American character. The story appeared in *Popular Magazine* with this editorial introduction: "The spirit of American democracy may have been born upon the battlefields of Concord and Lexington, but it grew to lusty manhood in these far reach-

es of the Columbia River, at the end of the Oregon Trail." David
Meriwether, dressed in fashionable eastern clothes, arrives in Oregon by
ship in search of his brother Elston. His mission is to persuade Elston,
who has been in the West nine years, to return to New York to help run
the family shipping business. Instead, he is initiated into the freedom
and vitality of western life, with its democratic individualism and self-
sufficiency. When he changes into buckskin clothes and moccasins, he
has the "startling sensation of changing characters, of dropping inward
restrictions and outward commandments." After shooting his first deer,
he smells the blood and realizes he has made a kill with his own arm and
eye. "The power of life and death was in him; he had discovered an
unknown ability, a new means of self-reliance." Following a ritualistic
fistfight to prove himself to the pioneer woman he is drawn to, he tells
his brother to burn his eastern suit; he is staying. Not much subtlety
here, just direct message: egalitarianism, self-reliant individualism, the
inevitability of violence, and the necessity to struggle in order to achieve
self-respect and control one's destiny.

At the end of his life, Haycox was writing about the same time, region,
and values, just doing it better. The contrasting values of East and West
on which this story pivots are, of course, a fundamental and recurrent
subject in westerns. But for Haycox the theme was more than mere convention. He exploited for literary purposes an idealized code of the West,
but he genuinely cherished the values he believed to be at its core.

"The Code," published in *Frontier* (June 1926), is a more subtle and
successful treatment of the unwritten rules of western behavior. The
code of the title refers specifically to the rule of minding one's own business but applies also to the general patterns of conduct distinctive of the
West. An old mountain man named Gabe Pilcher is loafing in front of a
saloon in Dodge, Kansas. Elvy Smeed, the saloon owner, trips over him
and begins to rough him up. A tall, good-natured cowboy steps in and
disposes of Smeed and takes Gabe in for drinks, saving the old man's
pride by saying he only interfered when he saw that Smeed was carrying
a gun and Gabe wasn't. Gabe is old, a drinker, full of stories of the era of
trapping and exploring, which nobody wants to listen to. The cowboy
does listen and treats him with respect. The cowboy gets in a poker
game and wins, even against Smeed's crooked gambler. Gabe observes.
He sees Smeed instruct a pair of hired killers. He wants to warn the cowboy, but doesn't want to violate the code of staying out of others' affairs.
He leaves with the cowboy and drops some hints, but the cowboy
doesn't encourage him. He goes back to the bar and tries unsuccessfully

to borrow a gun. Then he goes to where the cowboy has his horse and bedroll. He senses that the killers are close. As a way of warning the cowboy, he strikes a match. He is shot, but the cowboy is saved. The story has more weight and nuance than "Light of the West." The historical-cultural message is less explicit. In treating a violent episode in a trail town, Haycox is actually exploring the transition between the mountain men and the cattlemen, suggesting a link of continuity between the best of both. Gabe and the cowboy, with their mutual respect, represent a core tradition of the western spirit, and Gabe's giving his life for the cowboy has symbolic overtones.

Haycox's brief period in New York stimulated his interest in the Revolutionary War. For about a year he spent most weekends systematically visiting battlefields and historical points of interest in New York, New Jersey, Pennsylvania, Connecticut, and Massachusetts. The result was eight stories and two novelettes set during the American Revolution. The first of these was the novelette "Red Knives," published in the April 1925 issue of *Frontier*. George Rogers Clark and his rangers are in the Ohio frontier country in 1778. The fictional hero is sent by Clark on a spy mission to Detroit. This is romantic adventure of the great forest, much in the Cooper fashion. The level of plausibility is not high, but the action is swift and engaging. The love plot is conventional for such fiction: an unfortunate misunderstanding between lovers; chance brings them together in the wilderness; the villain kidnaps the heroine and chase and rescue follow. Some history and a patriotic message are tacked on. The diction is sometimes stilted: "a sinister chill of apprehension invaded him." The themes are overly explicit: "The hard frontier! It was not a life for soft men, and if frontier hearts were sometimes steeled beyond human compassion it was because inexorable forces so tempered them." And the patriotism is rather thick: with the information the hero brings back from his mission, "George Rogers Clark won the Northwest for a new and democratic nation."

The other novelette and stories appeared in *Adventure* between May 1926 and September 1928 and were eventually collected with an eye to the juvenile market in 1954 as *Winds of Rebellion: Tales of the American Revolution.*[18] They conform to a general pattern. Each deals with a major battle of the Revolution, and small maps are included to help the reader visualize the historical locations. The personal conflicts and adventures of fictional characters are interwoven with the battle events. A few historical figures play minor roles, with George Washington, in particular, appearing in the background as a revered, almost divine figure of leadership and purpose. But the focus is on the common soldier, and Haycox conveys the diversity among the troops from different regions as a way of showing how the glorious cause of independence welded them into a single nation. The influence of Cooper's *The Spy* is discernible in the plots and situations. The writing is improved over that of "Red Knives," demonstrating how quickly Haycox was learning his craft during this period. From the beginning he displayed considerable imagination in plotting and characterization. Style, diction, and the art of showing rather than explicitly stating came more gradually. These Revolutionary War stories provide, particularly for a young audience, a palatable blending of history, adventure, and patriotic message. And they display a certain amount of psychological complexity. Haycox was beginning to explore human motivations with more subtlety than did most pulp writers.

"A Battle Piece," first appearing in *Adventure* (23 September 1926), is representative of this cluster of stories. The historical focus is the first open and pitched battle of the Revolution. It was fought on Long Island in 1776, after the battle of Bunker Hill. General Howe leads the British, General Putnam the Continentals. A New Englander, Sergeant Abner Cotton, has brought a message to Putnam and is assigned to a unit from Maryland. Alex Carroll is singled out among the Marylanders. He is eager for battle, proud of his region, and contemptuous of New Englanders. He aims derogatory comments at Cotton. The latter was at Bunker Hill and thus has known some fighting. Cotton values camaraderie and would like to be accepted by the southerners. In the battle they are surrounded by three enemy units. Cotton and Carroll fight and die bravely, having gained a mutual respect for each other. Lying one upon the other in death, "they were now fellow members of a great company."

Haycox intended to write more about this era of America's history. He began a novel about Benedict Arnold but put it aside for some years. When he returned to it, he saw no need to complete it because by then Kenneth Roberts had published *Rabble in Arms*, a best-seller on the same subject.[19] He may also have felt disinclined to finish it because he had returned to the West and established himself so successfully in the western market. In any case, he learned at least two important things from writing about the Revolutionary War. The first was the importance of visiting locations and absorbing the distinctive qualities of a place. Those weekend excursions while living in New York began a habit of on-site research of the settings of his novels. The second lesson is revealed in this story Haycox told to an interviewer. His frequent walks in Prospect Park prompted him to write a story about the battle there. A reader in Baltimore wrote to him after the piece appeared saying that he had gotten the uniforms of the Baltimore troops wrong and had left out an old mill that had stood at the left of the battlefield. The man was a member of the Peabody Institute and knew what he was talking about. "That taught me a lesson. I went out and paid $35 for a rare book describing the uniforms of all Colonial troops, American, British, French, Hessian and so on. I haven't used the book since, but the investment was a sound one" (Wharton, 9). His library reveals that he continued buying such books in order to get historical details right. As for uniforms, his later descriptions of those worn by calvary in the West are precisely researched.

Exploring Western Formulas

From 1924 to 1927 Haycox published most frequently in *Western Story*. Then he switched to *Short Stories*, edited by Henry Maule. Perhaps Maule paid a better rate or allowed more flexibility in plotting and even an occasional paragraph of psychological or philosophical reflection. Whatever the reason, from July 1927 to June 1934, 45 Haycox short stories and novelettes appeared in *Short Stories,* and it was in this fiction that he established himself as a writer of category westerns and experimented with the various formulas of the cowboy story. Though still frequently using Oregon for his settings, he began writing about other specified and unspecified western regions. The lean, taciturn, slightly melancholy hero so typical of his novels began to emerge, along with his characteristic repertoire of sheriffs, villains, heroines, and plots. He employed established conventions, modified them, and sometimes invented new patterns. The extent to which he was imitating, refining, or inventing is difficult to determine because the volume of western fiction is so great and its formulas have always been in the public domain. There are no patents in fiction's cattle kingdom.

The pieces in *Short Stories* display plenty of variety but also considerable repetition in plot and characterization. Readers of magazine westerns did not want to read the same story repeatedly; they wanted to read the same *kind* of story. Haycox's gift from the beginning was a fertile imagination that enabled him to individuate basic plots freshly and create characters both individually interesting and formulaically functional.

The hero in these stories of the late 1920s is usually lean and weathered from days in the saddle, his muscles toned and elastic. He has an air of laconic certainty, a serene capability tempered by reserve, a confidence despite the knowledge that personal safety is always in doubt. This grace under pressure is regulated by a code of independent integrity and a respect for the same in others. He is peaceful and kind, but pushed by injustice, he can become a violent instrument of retribution: "Anger gleamed in his eyes, erasing the latent pleasantry, chiseling hard lines along his jaws. It made of him a gray and unforgiving man" ("Fandango," 25 October 1928). He is often a wanderer. If young, he has a reckless vitality that might lead him to either side of the law. If mature in experience even though not in years, he is slightly jaded by the familiar patterns of human conflict and violence. Young or seasoned, this wanderer is ripe for settling down when he encounters the right woman. She will set him on the right course if he is vacillating or give him purpose if he is world-weary. Until he finds that woman, male friendship is extremely important to him. Loyalty to friend or partner is a binding obligation. He attracts fiercely loyal friends who look to him for leadership. Sometimes an old friend will go bad and secretly involve himself in outlawry. The hero will be the last to credit rumors of such crookedness, and even though the friend will inevitably come to a bad end, the two will maintain a sort of mutual respect and loyalty. Increasingly, there is an element of naturalism in the characterization of these heroes that later, in his novels, became a Haycox trademark. Consider this reflection by the hero of "Secret River" (25 February 1928): "What was happiness, after all, but an illusive shadow which men ruined themselves in seeking? Hadn't everything in this vague world, from the highest star to the smallest form of life in the earth, told him time and time again that destiny marched on regardless of things living or dead? He was but an instrument moved by the supreme force that moved them all." This gloomy fatalism seems peculiar in a genre of invincible heroes and ineluctable happy endings, but it is ever present in Haycox's fiction, particularly in his last novel, lending his stories a certain weight uncharacteristic of popular fiction.

Many of the women in these stories exist simply to facilitate a happy ending and play no significant role in the action. Love at first sight is the rule, and the plots focus on conflicts between hero and villain rather than on the give and take of developing love relationships. But Haycox's treatment of women evolved in this group of stories. Alice Campbell of "Sevensticks Gamblers" (10 September 1928), for example, comes west on her own to avoid a marriage her family has planned for her. That prospect was too dull for her: "I could just see myself growing old, doing nothing. I guess I'm a gambler at heart." She provokes a young rancher into asserting himself against rustlers and actively assists him, at considerable personal risk. Often the women in these stories are trying to run ranches. They have inherited them or their fathers are weak and ineffectual. In either case, they must contend with a crooked foreman, their only support a faithful old family retainer, useful only for carrying messages. Haycox also began in these stories to use the device of two women as possible choices for the hero. The use of two heroines, one dark and one light, was a common convention of the nineteenth-century novel, used notably by Scott, Cooper, and Hawthorne.[20] In "Secret River" (25 February 1928) one is a schoolmistress from the East and the other a rancher's daughter. The situation here is simple and the choice obvious. The eastern woman is unsympathetically characterized as unable to appreciate western ways: "What a horrible, savage land! I never want to see it again. I never will!" Haycox continued to use the two-women device for the rest of his career, but with increasing complexity, exploring the many female permutations of dark and fair, East and West, passion and restraint, heart and head, aggressiveness and passivity, independence and submissiveness.

Even more common than the two-women pattern in these stories is the two-villain formula. The head villain is often a saloon owner, banker, or businessman in town who is secretly masterminding a gang of outlaws. His second in command is often a stocky, bullet-headed, bull-necked brute who provides the brawn to complement the ringleader's brains. The hero must possess both intelligence and physical strength to confront this evil duo, matching wits with the cunning boss, fists with the brutal henchman, and eventually guns with them both. The villains with intelligence evolve as Haycox works the formula. Some of the early ones display the unalloyed malignancy of melodrama. Gradually they are humanized and their evil given psychological explanation. The cold and deadly character of Jeff Sharp in "Starlight and Gunflame" (25 April 1928), for instance, is explained in this way: "Life is forever a lonely process; the most eloquent of men can translate only a beggar's mite of what moves inside him." Friendship can mitigate this situation, but Jeff had never known friendship; others were repelled by him. "If he could not command affection, could never join the camp fire circle, he could at least create a respect born of terror. . . . Being hated, he took to hating in turn." This is rudimentary psychology, but it makes the villain interesting. And even more interesting are the villains humanized enough to appear much like the heroes, possessing the same strengths and determination but oriented in the wrong direction. Later in his fiction Haycox went much further in exploring the good in evil men and the instincts for cruel violence in good men. These early stories intimate the direction of that exploration.

Sheriffs are another important element in his contributions to *Short Stories*. He developed a stock of lawmen. Many are dishonest, mere cat's-paws for villains or otherwise implicated in local outlawry. This is natural enough considering the nature of the genre. If sheriffs were honest and effective, what would be left for heroes to do? When the lawmen are honorable, they usually are the heroes, and several recognizable types emerge. One is the mild-mannered man with an aversion to bloodshed. He solves crimes and captures badmen using intelligence and cleverness; he's quick with his wits, not with his weapon. Several stories feature a lawman named Peach Murgatroyd (Haycox fills these stories with delightfully odd names—Craw Magoon, Slash Le Gore, Praygood Niggins, Rube Mamerock). In "Bandit from Paloma County" (10 May 1929) and "By Rope and Lead" (10 August 1929) Peach captures outlaws by ingenious tricks and without firing a shot. In "Powder Smoke" (10 September 1929), however, a sheriff friend engineers a situation in which Peach must use his gun. "A peace officer's got to be able to do that," he explains to Peach afterward. Before the showdown, Peach says to the woman with him, "This lead slingin' I never did like. Hate to die myself and hate to see others kick the beam. But I guess it's come to that." This change for Peach indicates a change in the stories as a whole. Some of them are essentially comic, filled with humorous vernacular and spiced with relatively harmless violence. The stories gradually shift from Twainian frontier humor to the formulas of fatal showdowns.

Two other types of lawmen deserve mention. There is the wise veteran sheriff who maintains a low profile and patiently allows events to work to his advantage. Canny in the ways of human nature, he sometimes bends the law to benefit a reckless youth at the crossroads of law and lawlessness. And there is Billy McGrane, featured in three stories. Nicknamed Bully, he maintains order in the toughest kind of town by sheer force and intimidation: "He was a massive, scowling, beetling creature, and he looked like John L. Sullivan, with whom, indeed, he once had sparred" ("Old Tough Heart," 25 March 1931). "McGrane took savage pleasure in making others hate him, in making others writhe under his hard dominance and at last desperately and futilely strike back. . . . Bully McGrane had only one thread of philosophy in his bruiser's head; might made right. And so while they cursed him, he sat back as some giant mastiff and jeered them with an arrogant, contemptuous indifference" ("Bully McGrane," 25 November 1930). The town fears and dislikes him but can't do without him. The older, cantankerous John Wayne would be perfect casting for this hard-boiled marshall. Of course, rigorously concealed beneath the hardness is a vein of sentiment that prompts him grudgingly and with embarrassment to kindness toward the helpless. The McGrane stories are humorous. Later, in *Trail Town*, Haycox modified the character for serious purposes.

Among the other types and patterns Haycox drew upon repeatedly for his *Short Stories* fiction are the following. The sneaky town informer who furnishes information to outlaws is a useful plot device. The gambler, whose avatar is Bret Harte's Oakhurst in "The Outcasts of Poker Flats," provides psychological variety. Educated and refined to the point of cynicism, he usually has a broken marriage in his past and a daughter he tries to look out for from behind the scenes. His compulsive gambling implicates him in the world of outlaws, but he maintains a flickering sense of honor. Haycox later developed this type to near tragic dimensions in such novels as *Alder Gulch*, *Trouble Shooter*, and *Trail Town*. Feuding families appear frequently, with young lovers from opposing clans. Outlaw towns—remote and scruffy places providing sanctuary for bad men—are locations of danger and challenge for the heroes. Fistfights are common, of course, and serve as an index both to physical strength and moral character. Dialogue is generously sprinkled with imagery from poker, that western game of games.

But while Haycox used formulas in plot and character in these stories, his settings are never generic. He visualized locations in concrete and particularized ways. There are, however, recurrent attitudes expressed in his descriptions of nature. Descriptions of the night sky in these stories indicate a pattern that increasingly became more frequent and pronounced in his fiction. For example, the hero of "Secret River" (25 February 1928) rides the trail at night, "and once again the unfathomed immensity of the sky, the sweet smell of sage, and the solace and mystery of the deep night were wrapping around him and tugging at his spirit." Mystery, solace, the insignificance of human actions within the cosmic scheme and yet intimations of meaning and a sense of well-being—these are the recurring elements of Haycox's night descriptions, and such passages constitute a sort of metaphysical core for his fiction. In them he is most tempted toward philosophical reflection.

The Breedlove-Bowers Stories

The preceding summary of the formulaic aspects of the fiction Haycox published in *Short Stories* may convey the impression that these stories are all standard cowboy action adventure. This is not true. Some of them are comic tales in the frontier humor vein. Owen Wister's *The Virginian*, the prototypical western, included, it should be remembered, the language, practical jokes, and oral storytelling characteristic of a major native tradition in American humor—the tradition born in the old Southwest, perfected by Twain, and still discernible in the outdoor sketches of Patrick McManus. During his apprenticeship in the pulps, Haycox was as much interested in western humor as in western heroism. Critics who find him lacking in humor are not giving the early stories their due. His success in the slicks entailed a filtering out of extravagant vernacular similes, dialect spellings, and the other features of frontier humor. Such features were common enough in *Collier's* and the *Post* in the 1920s but became less so later. During the 1930s the prose of western stories, like that of detective stories, lost much of its sentimentalism and ornament. Haycox's writing accordingly became more sober, and his success drew others in the same direction.

The use of a colloquial style and a delight in colorful language are, as Cynthia S. Hamilton explains, important aspects of the western: "Such a style proclaims a linguistic democracy where all are equal, and upholds democratic informality. The colloquial voice does this assertively, in the best brash American tradition." But, according to Hamilton, using the colorful vernacular presents a challenge. On the one hand, westerns tend to sentimentally and elegiacally glorify the West, glossing over controversy and contradiction. On the other, colloquial humor is undercutting, deflationary, and unsentimental. "There is delight in exposing contradictions, hypocrisy and pomposity, and often a sting, a wry twist intended to shock the reader or listener." The tension between these two directions can cause the writer trouble. She suggests that few westerns realize the artistic potential of the colloquial style: "Most flourish their dialect writing with a mixture of embarrassment over its vulgarity and triumph over its boldness, using it as an object for attention rather than as an artistic medium" (Hamilton, 37–39). In the late 1920s and early 1930s Haycox used the style and conventions of frontier humor with great success, and their disappearance in his later fiction is regrettable.

Haycox's first two contributions to *Short Stories* illustrate the two directions (humor and formulaic action) his talents and interests opened to him as he tried to make a good living writing about the West. The first story, "The Belle of Sevensticks" (25 July 1927), is entirely comic in the frontier vernacular manner—no hero, heroine, villain, sheriff, or action formula. Tully Bragg, a storekeeper, suggests that Sevensticks have a celebration to compete with a rival town's successful rodeo. He has in mind a festival to celebrate pioneers, a festival that would include a beauty queen. Hank Navin is skeptical and predicts that the rival town of Powder will have the last laugh. The plan stipulates that the queen will be provided by Powder and will be given satin shoes and promised three proposals of marriage before she leaves town. When the day arrives, citizens of Powder are conspicuous by their absence. Their queen arrives by stagecoach, having driven it part of the way herself, much to the consternation of the professional driver. The narrator provides this description of her arrival:

> I guess this yere lady had seen at least two generations mature an' fade while she was takin' root in our kindly soil. It is pretty cert'n she nev' had missed a square meal in thirty-forty years 'cause she stood a good seventeen hands from fetlock to ears an' she was durn near as solid aroun' the shoulders as my freightin' hosses, with a real fresh color in her cheeks. I wuldn' care to estimate her dead weight but I shore did see the stage coach sag an' bounce back when she trips lightly offen the steps an' hits the sand with grace enough to raise of young cloud o' dust.

Hank, who had earlier scoffed at the whole plan, is not laughing. She reminds him of his dead wife, and after she single-handedly stops a runaway six-horse team, he proposes. Told in colorful slang and dialect to a stranger, this is a frame story in the old Southwest humor style—comic similes, dialect spelling, juxtaposed incongruities, oral-tale flavor, and so on. It has a touch of comic genius and rivals Twain at his best. His affinity for humorous western vernacular was stimulated in his college years by assignments from W. F. G. Thacher to study such language in current magazines. Haycox began recommending notable examples to Arthur J. Larson, a fraternity brother with whom he carried on a lively correspondence in western colloquial lingo, addressing Larson as "Two Gun" and signing himself "Silent." His fiction in *Short Stories* is filled with earthy figures of speech. Here are some samples from "The Return of a Fighter" (10 October 1929): "Can allus tell a singed duck by the way it quacks"; "You sound better to me than eight banjos playin' the fandango"; "You boys ain't got any more business in this mess than a cockroach in soup"; "Hell's loose from its picket"; "And that gal will give you away like a shirt full o' fleas"; "Every dawg has a couple of good barks at the moon"; "That gent is smoother'n a peeled onion."

In sharp contrast to the first story, the second, "A Rider of the High Mesa" (25 September 1927), is an action novelette filled with trite formula elements. The heroine has no role except as reward for the hero at the end. Everyone suspects the hero of being crooked, but he is actually working undercover for the good of the community. The villain is a fat, wicked stereotype with designs on the heroine. The narrative employs many of the clichés of low-grade pulp adventure, including fortuitous eavesdropping, the ruse of conveying the impression that the hero is dead so that he can work behind the scenes, and even the old look-behind-you trick. The mystery and suspense are inadequately plausible because plot outstrips characterization. The hero seems rather dense to be so long in identifying the head villain, and the narrative withholds information in too contrived a way. This is perhaps as close as Haycox came to the inferior techniques of western formula. He would continue to use the formulas but shun the cheap narrative tricks.

The best of his stories in *Short Stories* combine the two threads of vernacular humor and action formula. The nine featuring Joe Breedlove and Indigo Bowers represent the best of Haycox's achievement in the pulps. The humor is engaging, the formulas are imaginatively modified, and the characters are interesting and credible.

Joe Breedlove first appears in the novelette "The Octopus of Pilgrim Valley" as a secondary character who aids a young hero.[21] The six chapters of the story each bear as an epigraph a bit of folksy wisdom quoted from Joe Breedlove. Twain used a similar device in *Pudd'nhead Wilson*. This is the only time Haycox used it. Breedlove seems to have been conceived as a humorous frontier philosopher, a colloquial commentator on human nature in its western setting. Haycox may even have envisioned him as a sidekick for the young hero. The wandering cowboy hero and sidekick was a popular pattern in the pulps and in the films they inspired. Whatever its origin, Haycox's conception of Joe Breedlove quickly changed. "Bound South," appearing just two months after "The Octopus of Pilgrim Valley," began a series of eight stories involving Breedlove himself as the wandering cowboy with a partner named Indigo Bowers.[22] These stories skillfully blend frontier humor with action and romance formulas, the humor and characterization being just as important as the action.

The charm of the Breedlove-Bowers stories lies mainly in the interaction between these two opposite but complementary personalities. Joe Breedlove, as his name implies, is amiable and well-disposed toward the world. He has a serenity, mellowness, and whimsicality about him that create affection and respect. He is tall and handsome, with a winning smile. He loves life but is never fooled by it. He is perceptive and thoughtful but never embittered. Knowing the devious ways of the world, he won't let that knowledge sour him. He moves lazily and speaks with a drawling gentleness, a trait that becomes more pronounced when he is roused. He is slow to take offense because he makes allowances for all frail, mortal things, but when roused by cruelty or injustice, he can be dangerous and volcanic. He is a man of much experience and discretion, swept clean of youthful egotism and intolerance. He seems older that his 35 years, partly because his temples are slightly silvered. And there is a touch of sadness about this shrewd observer of life. He has fond memories of a childhood in Kansas, but he began wandering at 14 and since then has known no real home. His ample charity is tempered by a concealed loneliness; his own youthful dreams have settled in the dust of the trail.

His partner, Indigo Bowers, is his opposite in most ways. Indigo's name suggests his blue temperament. He has an abiding distrust of the world and views life as one dirty trick after another. It is a point of pride with him never to admit that anything is exactly right; even the best things contain a catch. He is sensitive to all manner and forms of real and alleged injustice, and his fertile mind "browses around for every succulent bud of possible grief and disaster." For him, "the world was a snare and delusion and life was one vast effort at maintaining a proper respect for his dignity." Diminutive in stature, weighing about 120 pounds, he is a dynamic fighting bantam, convinced that people are always trying to pick on him. He is constitutionally unable to stay out of a quarrel—his own or someone else's. He is as homely as Joe is handsome—red hair, peaked nose, enlarged Adam's apple, shrewish mouth, perpetual frown. Though given to humorously extravagant figures of speech, he is essentially without humor. But with all his cantankerousness, "under his vest he concealed, like some terrible and criminal weakness, an absolutely dollar-sound heart." He is fiercely loyal to Joe and jealous of the women who are naturally attracted to his partner's gentle, amiable strength.

They are a strangely mated pair, drawn together by some peculiar chemical affinity. Indigo likes to end matters as abruptly as possible, whereas Joe likes to "hemstitch a few artistic posies into human relations." They know each other thoroughly and can communicate in a crisis by the subtlest modulation of facial expression. They have thousands of miles behind them and no visible goal ahead: "These two were like work ponies turned out. They found the freedom good and they tarried at green pastures only for a night, avoiding all entangling fences, refusing every bait that led to a corral." As they become involved in the affairs of others in their travels, Joe works through humor, intelligence, and charm and often remedies situations with clever manipulation rather than with fist or gun. These stories display a hint of the picaresque tradition with its clever hero. Indigo, as sidekick, makes important contributions in these adventures. His function is not that of a Gabby Hayes or Andy Devine to provide bumbling, slapstick comic relief: he is a consummate fighter and strategist. This pair's adventures take them through the formulas already described, but the dialogue and characterization provide greater interest than the riding and shooting.

The First Three Novels

Haycox's first three novels—*Free Grass*, *Chaffee of Roaring Horse*, and *Whispering Range*—were serialized in *West* between December 1928 and December 1930. They are formula westerns but display originality in conception and method. By this time Haycox knew his market expertly and conformed to the stereotyped and repetitive patterns it demanded, but he retained a sense of autonomy and an ambition for artistic development. This independence and drive produced stories that earned high praise in the pulp field and distinguished him from the mass of anonymous hacks. He chafed under the strictures of magazine publishing, but the commercial market brought him recognition and financial security he was loath to relinquish for the uncertainties and modest earnings of book publishing. He viewed magazine serialization as preliminary to book publication, but preliminary in a very important financial sense. A serial was fairly lucrative; a book—unless lightning struck—was not. For example, he confided to Thacher that he expected his first book to earn only about $400 from sales of 2,000 to 3,000 copies.[23] Being a practical professional, he compromised by continuing to use the formulas while simultaneously trying to invest them with greater artistic skill and significance. And, at least in the beginning, he may have humored himself into believing that writing novels, even for a pulp magazine, would allow for some artistic scope.

Haycox was not alone in attempting this compromise. The main subject of Christine Bold's *Selling of the Wild West* is the friction created when an author of westerns tries to create some variation in the formula: "From time to time throughout the decades of the formulaic Western's popularity, certain authors implanted in their presentation of conventional plots signs of either their own authorial individuality, or their attempts to transcend the limitations of the genre, or their defiance of patterning. In every case, the form of the popular Western tells a more individual and unpredictable story than does its content" (Bold, xi). But Haycox is certainly a notable case of a gifted writer who produced formulaic fiction for profitable returns while at the same time trying to satisfy his artistic ambitions by experimenting with narrative techniques that give his stereotyped material a degree of subtlety and literary artistry. These limited inventions were a way of constantly trying to expand the artistic latitude allowed by the restraining supervision of commercial editors. This experimenting gave him, at least temporarily, some sense of artistic development.

A week before Doubleday, Doran published *Free Grass* in February 1929, Haycox wrote to Thacher requesting that he arrange to have the book reviewed in the *Emerald*, the University of Oregon newspaper. He describes the novel as "slightly historical, in which I find I do my best, though the history won't impede the skip and run reader any. It's a trail herd and new soil yarn. [Emerson] Hough brought the trail herd from Texas to Abilene. I am taking the herd from Dodge City on north to Dakota. Plenty of adwentoor, much of those romance, a few very, very dirty guys. Extremely dirty. And some humor and some landscape. There she lies." It is a western, he says, "but I tried to write it with some reverse English." He also suggests that he might be interviewed in connection with the review. "In that interview I'd scorch Mr. Albert Richard Wetjen's point of view [that pulp fiction is devoid of artistic merit] for some number of words. Dick and I have battled it out privately and a little publicly printed friction wouldn't hurt at all." Then, after describing the splintering and unstable condition of the pulp market, he states his plans: first, to "climb out of the pulps to white paper and try to get a steady berth. Second, plug at novels and work them up to a decent sale."[24]

His description of *Free Grass* is playful, but that is simply his characteristic modesty. Though he took his writing very seriously, he always spoke about it with playful self-deprecation. The phrase about trying to write with reverse English hints at how carefully and ambitiously he had approached this first novel. The reference to Wetjen is a clue leading in the same direction. Wetjen wrote sea novels and aspired to be another Conrad. He had what a friend called a "genius complex," an exaggerated estimate of his own talent sustained by downgrading the talent of others. He was condescending toward pulp writers, though he published in that field "just for the money" and obviously was jealous of Haycox's energy and success. He found Portland provincial and disparaged

Haycox for being satisfied there. He assumed a bohemian pose and made snide remarks about Haycox being a Republican and Rotarian. Haycox probably desired to answer Wetjen at this point because he had just completed a novel he was proud of. It had appeared in a pulp magazine, but he felt it had some artistic merit, and now it would appear in hardcover. As for his plan to climb out of the pulps into a steady place in the slicks, he accomplished that two years later by becoming a *Collier's* regular. And he plugged at novels by publishing about one a year for the next 20 years.

We can only guess what he meant by using reverse English in writing *Free Grass*, but the technique that stands out is an extensive and intricate elaboration of theme. This distinguishes the novel from the usual western of the time and even from Haycox's subsequent novels. *Free Grass* examines the western code explicitly and from several perspectives. It is as though Haycox used his first novel as an opportunity to treat ideas and establish a unifying philosophical viewpoint in ways unavailable to him in his previous short fiction.

Tom Gillette, a young Texan who has just finished five years of education in the East, returns with an eastern friend, Claude Lispenard, to the West, meeting his father's trail herd in Dodge to help move it to the Dakotas. Tom is ennobled by casting off his Eastern ways and embracing the western code. His friend's character, on the other hand, degenerates in the western environment. Two women are involved—the pattern Haycox had used before in his short fiction and continued to use almost obsessively in his novels, and used effectively enough to be widely imitated. In this instance the pattern is simple. Kit Ballard is a sophisticated New Yorker. Regretting that she had toyed with Tom's heart in the East, she follows him West with the intention of winning him and helping him achieve wealth or political position in the East. Lorena Wyatt is a cattleman's daughter who rides and ropes with the best of the hired hands. She embodies the code, and Tom must fulfill the code to win her. His choice between the women is never in doubt because the novel is obviously slanted to favor the West over the East. The other major elements, as Haycox indicated to Thacher, are dirty guys, humor, and landscape. The principal dirty guy is San Saba. Described in imagery of shadows and darkness, he is the murderer of Tom's father and of course must fall to Tom's gun on the penultimate page. The humor is supplied by three vernacular tall tales distributed in the narrative. The landscape is the vast prairies, described with both accuracy and symbolic resonance.

The glorification of the code is embarrassingly explicit: "How strong
was the grip of the frontier code! A man must take care of his own quar-
rels, never delegate them. To shirk this was to confess weakness, and that
weakness would follow him like an accusing finger wherever he went."
The rules are few but immutable: "Never to go back on his word; to give
all humans the right to live the way they wished to live in return for the
same right to himself; to uphold this right with the last breath of his
body." This is the stuff of parody nowadays, and there is even a hint of
parody in Tom's first musings on the code when he is fresh from the East:
"Shoulder to shoulder, fist to fist. Play your own hand, ask no favors, ride
straight, shoot fast, keep all obligations." But the novel takes such customs of the country soberly. The code may have little to do with the actual West, but it has a great deal to do with the West of the imagination
and with Haycox Country in particular. Whether the code was reality or
myth or a little of both is beside the point in considering Haycox's artistic
ambitions in this first novel. The most interesting thing about *Free Grass*
is the way so many of its elements are designed to convey the East-West
contrast. The hero, first of all, is in conflict with himself, divided between
his eastern training and his western roots. This inner tension is compounded by the attraction of the eastern and western woman, and by the
fact that his friend, an easterner, degenerates in the West.

Tom's fistfight with Lispenard is symbolically not a battle between
East and West but a struggle between two responses to the nature of
western life. Lispenard's flawed character was held in check by eastern
restraints, but western freedom allows it to fester and destroy him. He
becomes coarse and slovenly, both physically and morally. He is the type
of the frontier renegade who, trained to be civilized and knowing right
from wrong, still succumbs to the ways of animality opened by the frontier's lack of external restraints. Judging by eastern standards, he mistakes the quite different but no less binding western manners for no
manners at all. In San Saba, Tom confronts a western villain; in
Lispenard, a perversely westernized eastern villain. In addition, he con-
tends with Barron Grist, an easterner representing a corrupt eastern land
company. The East-West permutations are intricately conceived. Even the
humor, the tall tales, function to accentuate regional differences. The
same is true of landscape. Kit finds the landscape too raw and ungener-
ous; it makes her feel small and insignificant. Tom thinks there is nothing
wrong with that feeling: "In the East folks lose sight of the truth. Inside a
house they're little tin gods—but the house makes a servant of 'em. Out
here we walk abroad. We know we're small potatoes, but we're free."

In short, Haycox's principal achievement in this first novel was to succeed with action formula while at the same time directing language, plot, characterization, setting, and even humor to the exploration and exposition of theme. His literary aspiration was asserting itself at its first sustained opportunity, even though he recognized he was working under constraints. He told his friend and fellow writer Charles Alexander that "the thin part of the book is of course the plot, which of necessity had to follow along conventional lines. And this will continue to be the thin part of my stories until I can afford to wean myself from serial rights in the pulps. Then we shall see."[25] Actually, sophisticated development of theme was not the proper avenue for a writer of magazine action adventure, in the pulps or the slicks. Nothing should hinder or detract from narrative movement. Haycox had to face this as he continued writing novels for magazine serialization, and he gradually backed away from emphasizing themes and ideas in his serials, confining most of his artistic experimentation to the short stories, for which editors were less insistent about action formula. For Haycox the aspiring artist, western serials would be restrictive. On the other hand, for Haycox the craftsman, they still allowed opportunities for growth. He found within the constraints of the magazine market room to perfect important writing skills. For the next 15 years, despite a perpetual desire to attempt more profound literary feats, he accepted the role of craftsman and established a reputation as a writer of superior westerns.

The letter to Alexander just quoted clearly reveals the competing impulses within Haycox: toward a profitable living as a magazine writer, on the one hand, and toward artistic quality on the other. The phrase "then we shall see" gnawed at him until he finally divorced himself from the serial market in the late 1940s. He goes on in the letter to say, "Novel number Two is just beginning to throw off sparks in my head. I hope to have it done in six months. And I want it to be both longer and more human and thicker than the present one." This is the aspiring literary artist speaking, but immediately the magazine craftsman breaks in: "And more entertaining. That's fundamental. We write to entertain. In short, my motto is the same as that of Wilkie Collins—make 'em laugh, make 'em weep, make 'em wait." Then in the next sentence he switches back to artistic ambitions: "The background of the next novel is to be the pressure of the land itself on the characters. Folks can talk of the inexorable, etc. qualities of the sea, but the sea hasn't had one twentieth of the influence in shaping and warping and defeating man that the land has. The sea is only more spectacular about it. One can leave the sea." Perhaps his rivalry with Wetjen was in the corner of his mind in this reference to sea stories. In any case, the talk of great forces shaping, warping, and defeating man seems incongruously juxtaposed with the motto "make 'em laugh, make 'em weep, make 'em wait." He was a divided writer, and whatever his achievement, it resulted from a continual inner process of negotiation and compromise.

The second novel, *Chaffee of Roaring Horse*, has more action than *Free Grass,* and maybe that is what Haycox had in mind for making it more entertaining. The hero is forced off a cliff in a stampede, runs a violent stretch of white water river in a rowboat (an original touch), nearly freezes in a mountain pass, is jailed and breaks out, solves a murder mystery, jails the cunning master villain, and shoots the brute of a henchman. There is an underlying theme, but it is less obtrusive than in *Free Grass*. It is the conflict between the populist values of individualism and private property and the forces of change, capitalistic development, and alleged progress. The East-West dichotomy of *Free Grass* is modulated. The corrupt capitalistic land scheme that had its source and impetus in the East in the first novel is now endemic to the West. The heroine is a product of both regions and combines the best qualities of each.

At this stage of his career, Haycox's keen interest in characterization manifests itself in several advances over his beginning work. The heroine is a substantial and interesting character. A freelance investigator with a clouded past, she is independent, resourceful, and has "a store of experience surpassing that of many a man." Without trying to play the role of good fellow among men, she seems unself-conscious about her sex. She takes a significant part in the action and even saves the hero's life. The principal villain is also portrayed with psychological depth. He combines qualities of East and West in a distinctive mix. His house reflects his cultivated tastes and his ambition. He has an "autocratic and arbitrary mandarin spirit," a phrase illustrating that Haycox refused to write down to his readers; his fiction displays an unusually ample vocabulary range for this genre.

His preoccupation with human variety and uniqueness is revealed particularly in a distinctive array of minor characters. A notable example is Mark Eagle, an Umatilla Indian educated in a government school and now working as a bank clerk. He discovers he has no satisfying place in either the Anglo or Native American world. His portrayal is as sympathetic and relevant as the most recent public television documentary on the subject. Haycox, though schooled in the pulp writing of the 1920s, was uninfected by its frequent racism. Edison Marshall, his model of success while a student at the University of Oregon, wrote passages like this one describing his hero and heroine: "With such companionship as they had, as existed everywhere between well-mated men and women of their race, what heathen hordes could conquer them, what lesser breeds despoil them of their dominance."[26] Haycox made a career of delineating heroic strength, but he never made it a matter of race or sex.

The impact of land upon character mentioned in the letter to Alexander does not come into play as much in *Chaffee of Roaring Horse* as in the third novel, *Whispering Range*. Landscape in the second novel is treated much as in the first: with a sense of wonder, reverence, and humility. The precipitous gorge of the Roaring Horse River enthralls the young lovers with "the eternal lure of the mystery of life." The forces of nature in *Whispering Range*, however, are harsh and adversarial. The main character had since childhood "been fighting savagely against the dominant elements. His whole life had been fashioned and tempered by these struggles and so now in manhood David Denver looked on the wild forces of nature as a pagan would, endowing these forces almost with living personalities," prizing any victory in "that everlasting skirmish with the earth." Faced with the necessity of crossing a flooded river, Dave is roused, his eyes "flared with the morose desire to check and defeat that overwhelming, inevitable power under the shadow of which all men walked. Burning sun, blizzard, miring mud, snow-choked trails, thirst, starvation—he had fought these things doggedly, and now he found the same grim, impersonal enemy in front of him again, shaped as a swollen river." Related to the forces of nature in this third novel is the power of fate. Dave is gripped by "a sense of being inevitably pushed on toward a long-prepared-for crisis in his life; a crisis made not by man but by a force beyond man's control." This element of fate became a frequent part of Haycox fiction but never the whole story: free-willed responsibility ultimately triumphs in a freedom-versus-fate struggle that Haycox often made convincing and even moving.

The man and nature, freedom and fate, conflicts of the novel are complemented by a tension between self and society. Dave begins as a lonely, rebellious individualist, opposed to mass action, so strongly independent that he is caught between outlaw and vigilante factions. He thinks, "I despise posses about as much as I despise outlaws. Who is to say whether the man hunted is so much blacker than the man hunting? Who is to be judge?" Like the hero of *Free Grass*, he wants to "let every man stand responsible for his acts, and let every man fight his own fights." This, as Haycox taught us in that first novel, is the essence of the code. But now his hero realizes that this "is something soon enough impossible to do. Then what?" Dave is forced to choose. He wanted to live and let live and not judge others, but he can't escape the clear call of conscience and must take collective action. Injured and dependent on others, he realizes something has been missing in his life. This is also the turning point in the love story because he recognizes his need for a woman's love. His resistance to society is skillfully counterpointed by a psychologically complex villain who uses a similar refusal to run with the pack as a rationalization for his evil. The code, so explicitly glorified in *Free Grass*, becomes the focus for probing moral ambiguity in this novel. Al Niland, Dave's friend and a voice of moral commentary in the novel, provides a paragraph on moral complexity, the upshot of which is that "man builds up a pretty schedule of ideals—and life knocks it flatter than a pancake." He later adds, "Nobody can live a useful life without gettin' dirty. Moses broke half of his own commandments." Moral ambiguity continued to preoccupy Haycox, even as he used the alleged morally simplistic western formulas.

The texture of ambiguity in *Whispering Range* is rich in several of the novel's aspects: the hero's inner conflict, the psychology of the villain, the relationship between hero and villain, and the attraction presented by the two women, Eve Leverage and Lola Monterey. The choice between these two women is much less obvious than in earlier stories. When Lola and Eve frankly discuss Dave, Lola says, "You are one thing—I am another. Perhaps if both our natures were in one woman Dave would puzzle himself no longer." As it turns out, Eve has a little of Lola hidden inside, which she reveals only gradually. The passionate Lola desires too much of Dave and offers herself to him too aggressively. Eve better understands his need for autonomy and patiently holds herself back while he discovers his need for her. Haycox enlarges his formula by using a small subplot to reinforce the idea that a woman should not interfere too much with a man's individuality. Dave's friend Steve Steers's relationship with Debbie Lunt is not satisfactory until Steve insists upon this point.

The use of a subplot is linked with an increase in the number of characters in this novel. More characters and subplots became one of Haycox's distinctive contributions to enlarging the western formula. Another example of this enlargement in *Whispering Range* is a very minor subplot in which Fleabite Wilgus goes to court over an old horse, wins the case, but the horse has died during the trial. This is frontier humor used simply as comic relief. Two other comic characters, Wango and

Meems, ne'er-do-well cowboy loiterers about town, serve a more important narrative function by providing useful commentary on the action. Another fresh and interesting minor character is a highly educated Englishman who at first appears to be the stock greenhorn, a brunt for practical jokes, but who turns out to be shrewd and capable.

Whispering Range is an admirable culmination to Haycox's career in the pulps. Though not his last piece for this market, it is his best. And it was well received as a book, selling 6,000 copies in the first printing, which is three times that of the first printing of *Free Grass* (Etulain 1966, 97).

A letter to Alexander in 1931, thanking him for reviewing *Whispering Range*, reveals Haycox's state of mind regarding his writing at the end of his 10-year apprenticeship in the pulps. He begins with an observation on the general difficulty of capturing an imaginative conception in written words: "Nobody knows quite so well as I do, how hellishing wide of the mark I write most of the time. You and I both know that if we could get on paper the real vividness and heat of what went racing through our minds we'd begin to be actual storytellers. It's a discouraging business. When a tale is told it is only the wreckage of a fine idea." These are not the words of a complacent pulp hack. He then reflects on how his most recent novel measures up to his aspirations:

I liked *Whispering Range* better than some of the stories I've done, in spite of the fact it's undoubtedly haywire in parts. The same old atmosphere is there and much of the same old business. But then, that's true of *Lorna Doone*, *Pilgrim's Progress* and *The Odyssey*. Nothing counts but character; or, to be more exact, nothing counts as much as that. I spread myself in the book to outline more figures and get them a little away from type. I was disappointed in Denver; he's only one third the man I'd hoped he'd be. Originally he was going to be a full pagan, earth-worshipper. And originally the sun and the blizzard, the mud and the freshet would have made up the dominating force of the piece. But you kain't do that in westerns. So I was up a creek with no oars in hand. One thing I'm tired of is the *The Virginian* type of hero, even though I'll use him ten thousand times again. I wanted Denver to be unorthodox. But the odd thing is, few people like the one character I'd throw away the rest of the book for—Lola. Eve Leverage isn't much, but dammit Lola's got melody in her. In all the thousands of words of nonsense I've written, she's one of the three or four characters I ever cared much about. But that's usual. Nobody loves the author's loves. . . . One guy said he smelled Hardy faintly. That made me mad—for the original story would have been five times {as} Hardyesque as the final transcription. But as I say, you kain't do that in westerns. Well, someday, Charley, I'll write a book. You can't keep a fellow from hoping.[27]

At this point in his career, Haycox knew from diligent practice the difficulties of the art of fiction, yet his enthusiasm to confront the challenges had in no way diminished. The letter to Alexander also indicates his uneasy accommodation with the commercial market: his hope that characterization could redeem formula, his desire to enlarge and vary the types, his interest in more complete female characters, his frustration at having to rein in his artistic ideas, and his consoling trust that the future would bring new opportunities for more self-fulfilling achievement.

Chapter Three

From Rough Page to Smooth

The Transition to *Collier's*

Haycox's important move from pulp magazines to *Collier's* resulted from a combination of effort, achievement, and simple luck. Throughout the 1920s he had submitted stories to *Collier's* without success. Meanwhile, he was earning an increasingly good living in the pulps. This suddenly changed with the economic crash of 1929, which forced pulp editors to cut back acceptances and rates of payment. Haycox was in the process of paying for a house, car, and other goods his prosperity had led him to buy, and for a while his financial prospects were alarming. Richard Wetjen later described Haycox's plight to John Hawkins: "When I said that Haycox was a superb example of calmness and assurance I didn't count in the sweats he went through when he had to make the slicks or starve, the pulp markets being shot in the great days of '30. That, I think, was his only moment of real qualm. . . . [T]here's no doubt that for a year or so he was hanging on the ropes."[1] Fortunately for Haycox, *Collier's* at this same time had lost one of its best writers of outdoor adventure and badly needed a replacement. This magazine had become the chief rival of the *Saturday Evening Post* and had increased its circulation from 1.5 million to nearly 2.5 million between 1927 and 1931.[2] Because its audience was largely men, male-directed action fiction was an important component in its success. It liked to use established names and use them regularly. Haycox had made a prominent mark in the pulps and was a likely candidate. *Collier's* wired him for a submission and accepted it. It was a story written for the pulps and not really among the best he had done for that market. He recognized the irony of his good fortune: after 10 years of trying to break into the slicks, he backed into *Collier's* with a mediocre story intended for the pulps.

But this occurrence is not surprising. By 1930 western fiction in the pulps and slicks was becoming increasingly indistinguishable, and some writers were moving freely from one outlet to the other. Haycox, for example, published his first story in *Collier's* in February 1931 and

appeared regularly in its pages until 1949, but he continued writing for
the pulps until 1934. His letters in 1931 reveal the nature of his transition from rough to smooth pages. To Arthur B. Epperson he wrote, "For
your information and guidance I'll say you will see less and less of me in
Short Stories or *West*; and more of me in *Collier's, Ace-High*. To which I
may add you'll possibly see me in *Argosy, Western Stories*—and one of the
very biggest boys in the country which I shan't name until I know
more."[3] The big boy was obviously the *Post*, his debut in which was still
12 years away. In a letter to his brother-in-law, he reviewed his first 10
years of writing: "The first year I made about $60. The second some-
where around $200. The third year $2,076. The fourth $3,034. The
fifth $4,099. The sixth $5,910. And so on, far into the night. This last
year I took in almost an exact $12,000. But in 1931 I won't equal it for
several reasons; first, because the market's bad and second because I'm
riding two horses instead of one—that is, I'm trying to make the big
boys and the number of rejections will eat up a large part of the profit
from the pulp market."[4] This financial report to a family member indicates that writing was a practical matter of business to him and that
moving from one market to another was a calculated risk.

Breaking into the slicks was a watershed in his career, but it compounded his vacillation between financial and artistic goals. He had
anticipated that writing for *Collier's* would immediately allow him
greater artistic latitude. This hope was soon disappointed. As he later
explained to Thacher,

> That first story I sold to Collier's was one I had written for the pulps.
> When it was accepted and they asked for more, I said to myself, "You're
> in the slicks now, old boy. You don't have to stick so closely to formula.
> You can indulge in a little verbal imagery once in a while. Or give your
> characters a twist of psychology. Or even editorialize a bit." I wrote my
> next stories with that in mind—and darned if they didn't come back.
> "All right, gentlemen," I said, "I can take a hint. If it's a story told
> *straight* that you want, that's what you'll get." And I haven't had a rejec-
> tion since.[5]

The last part of this statement might suggest that he was resigned to
conforming to formula for the sake of financial security. This is only
partly true. From 1931 to 1945 he became increasingly dissatisfied with
his repetitions. In his serials he added new but never very important
variations to his formula. His editors usually resisted anything more
than minor experiments. They were more accommodating with his

short stories, however, and he found some opportunities for artistic development in them, enough perhaps to keep his artistic ambitions alive and gnawing at him.

A long, candid letter to Thacher in 1932 reveals Haycox's ambitions. Although Thacher had done much to train him for popular magazine writing, Haycox also viewed his former teacher as a sort of artistic conscience. "You have always been more or less of a shadow behind me," he told him, "a pointing finger as it were—not accusing, but definitely demanding." He assumed that Thacher had been waiting for him to master his craft and then produce something significant:

> With you, there can be no question as to a writer's real aim, and no excuse if a writer does not utilize such gifts as he may possess toward the very highest end. Brush economics aside, and all the minor considerations that influence ordinary men—the writer must serve his functions. He has got to make the gamble, someday, even if it ruins him. I realize it. I know that for a man to go along on the even and safe schedule year after year is nothing less than an admission that he is a hack, that he does not belong in the great tradition. The spirit isn't in him. It goes back to a proposition I always have believed: No writer is a greater writer than he is a man. I do not mean necessarily the outward aspects of gentlemanliness. I mean the inward ferment and strength and boldness and toughness.[6]

Haycox may have been projecting his own literary ideals onto Thacher, who was hungry all his life for any kind of publication, never placing very much, and certainly never attempting serious literature. Some view him as a rather pathetic figure warming his own ego in the glow of Haycox's success. James Stevens and W. L. Davis satirize him in their 1927 pamphlet on the condition of Northwest literature, portraying him as a silly contributor to advertising slogan contests.[7] When he began a biography of Haycox after the latter's death, Jill, after consulting with some of Thacher's former students, put a stop to it. "It's rather sad," she said, "the poor old man wants so badly to see his name on a book."[8]

Haycox himself always viewed Thacher as a respected friend and advisor, sharing with him his deepest writing concerns and requesting his opinions on manuscripts, particularly late in his life when he gave up writing magazine serials to attempt historical novels. He confided to Thacher in 1937 that writing was a lonely life. He said he didn't mind that much because isolation has some compensations, but still he concluded that one needs someone on his own frequency: "If a man has at least one friend to whom he can lay out his thoughts without self-consciousness on either side he's very lucky. So I'm lucky. I don't know of any other man to whom I can write this freely."[9] Perhaps Haycox, needing such a literary confidant, created one in Thacher, seeing in him what he needed to see. Or it may be that he recognized qualities in Thacher that escaped others. In any case, their friendship was genuine and enduring.

Haycox goes on in the 1932 letter to share his artistic soul-searching: "I do not doubt. I am not afraid, and I have the same ambition that I had ten years ago. I have an unlimited faith in certain aspects of my writing. I'll stack my best lines of writing, for instance, against anybody writing today. Insofar as pure style is concerned, I'm not afraid." He admitted to an ample sense of ego, which, he said, a writer must have in abundance. And while he claimed to have put his ego into the written page rather than spending it in public, he admitted being sympathetic with the artistic temperament, even as manifested in Dreiser, Lewis, and Wetjen: "The potentially greatest writer in this state today is Dick Wetjen, not many stages removed from a bum. The necessary reckless-ness is in him." Haycox could admire that recklessness but was himself cautious. Even though he was confident about his style, he conceded uncertainty that he could "carry a big piece of work through." He said he doubted whether he was "well-enough bottomed now to sling a very heavy pen." He recognized how his views had been modified by ordinary experience and how he was building a reserve of knowledge "to color and strengthen—and sometimes to abate—my first conclusions." He said he didn't think he had a deep mind, nor does any writer: "It isn't our function." The writer excels not by profound intellect but by sensi-tivity to impressions and skill in creating illusions. He thought he had been continuously stretching: "I can handle more situations, more kinds of people; and I think I can do a better job. But some of my work is pretty pale. I'm not satisfied. I do not consider any writer to be such who is confined to one narrow field and is lost beyond it."

Haycox sensed a change in his writing. He couldn't go back to what he was doing three years ago. *Argosy* had just asked him for a straight western. Three years before he could have given them just what they wanted: "a surface story with just enough variation to give it some spice." But what was he writing? "A western yarn with an old plot com-pletely honeycombed with motive and aside-thoughts that will leave *Argosy* utterly disgusted. I think I have lost that $600. But I cannot write a surface story any more. So that's some progress, if we forget the $600, which is no simple trick." Apparently *Argosy* was not disgusted, or else he limited the motives and asides, because "The Hour of Fury" appeared in the 1 April 1933 issue. In looking ahead to the next four or five years, he predicted:

> I shall pass out of the heavy-stressed yarns of action and strong virile emotion. I shall no longer beat readers on the head. The next stage is something light and crisp, that says much in little, that is stronger illusion and less factual [this suggests the kind of fiction *Collier's* aimed for under the editorship of William Chenery]. These stories, mind you, will be no more valid, from the point of view of good writing, than the pulp stories; but they will be in *Collier's* and *Post* and *McCalls* and *Cosmo*. In those years I shall have made myself fairly independent, for the depression has taught me never again to go along without heavy cash reserves. Then—and this is the old theme without variation—we shall see.

He confessed that at this time money was a principal concern: "It may make me less of a writer, but I can't overlook the obligations I have. I can't overlook the matter of security for the family. As things now stand I should say that it will take me another five years to accomplish this much. I'll then be 38. So much for economics."

This letter amply reveals his state of mind as he made his transition to the slicks. The tensions and vacillations are obvious between confidence and doubt, complacency and ambition, security and risk, money and art, self-justification and guilt, modesty and egotism, pragmatism and esthetic temperament. This unsettled state perhaps sparked the following explosion of hyperbole in a letter to Arthur Epperson the same year: "This most competitive profession on earth has been a three-ringed circus, a comet shooting its way through some heavenly galaxy, four thousand fourth of Julys rolled in one, a madhouse of fifty thousand editors and writers in an iron cell cracking out a living with iron hammers; a confusion, a turmoil, and upheaval; a crying, a shouting, a long, shrill wailing; death and destruction, bereavement, suffering and oblivion."[10] This is playful exaggeration, but it was prompted by a genuine relief and heady excitement at breaking into *Collier's*.

The Man and the Routine

"Restraint is habitual with me," Haycox once wrote to Thacher. "I boil inside but am fairly placid outside."[11] The inner boiling was a fertile imagination generating the romance, conflict, and adventure that found expression in his fiction. The outer placidity was a rather uneventful life centered in regular work habits, home, family, and community service.

When his editor at Little, Brown requested more biographical information in 1939, he replied that there was little to provide: "Nothing ever happens to a writer—nothing important. All a writer is, anyway, is a large set of ears and a large set of eyes hooked up to an unstable nervous system. Primarily he's a recorder of events, almost never a doer. If he can do things, he can't write—and vice versa."[12]

James Fargo provides this description of Haycox's physical appearance: "He was of slender build without fat, a dapper dresser. A naturally high forehead accentuated by baldness gave his face a domed, thoughtful appearance. His nose was large, long, and blunt-tipped; his eyes deep brown with grooved crow's feet beside them from much smiling. His mouth seemed meant to grin; it was a wide mouth with full, sensuous lips that found repose only when curled around his pipe or his cigar." Another source describes him as a wiry type, fond of the outdoors, a hiker and skier with tanned face. "He had a habit of quickly compressing his lips just before speaking, and his voice was rather musical when he let the words ripple out, nicely picked and expressively given."[13] He apparently valued size in his possessions and owned a big house, big car, big boat, big garden, even big dogs (Saint Bernards); yet he was a modest man. Material success seemed not to turn his head; he was known affectionately for his naturalness, charm, and integrity. In his fiction the greedy accumulation of wealth is portrayed as the chief source of injustice in society and moral deterioration in the individual.

He imagined western adventure; he didn't live it. He loved hiking, camping, skiing, and visiting the locations he wrote about, but he was not a horseman and had little interest in guns and hunting. He liked outdoor work and work with his hands. From 1939 to 1940 he built a 30-room southern colonial mansion in the hills above Portland. When the builders finished, he began his own projects, beginning with an elaborate 400-square-foot chicken house, followed by a building of equal size called the "tool house," and finally a "pump house," which required for justification the drilling of a deep well. All these were his own work, while at the same time he was developing more than an acre of garden and orchard. This perpetual labor was done in the evenings and on weekends. He was sometimes mistaken for a hired man. He used some of those, too, but, according to his son, none matched his energy.[14] He always yearned to be a rancher or gentleman farmer, and in later years he bought a farm on the Willamette River, where he spent a lot of time, learning the hard truth that it was a costly venture.

Most of Haycox's time, however, was devoted to steady, methodical writing. Dressed immaculately, he went each weekday from nine to five to a small office in downtown Portland. Sitting at his desk with tie on and shirt sleeves to his wrists he wrote and did research. According to his son, he usually produced five pages of typescript a day on an aging Underwood upright with a left-hand carriage return. A secretary would retype this draft to be reviewed and edited the following morning. If he completed seven or eight pages, he was a little suspicious and usually had to do a good deal of next-day repairing (Haycox, Jr., vii). Years of conscious effort to put down the right word the first time enabled him for the most part to do so, but still he made numerous changes before he was satisfied.

Haycox didn't believe in inspiration and didn't wait for it. He simply went to his office, put paper in the typewriter, and made himself write. He thought writers are mostly made, not born. They must have an innate interest in words and a sense of dramatic values, but the rest can be achieved through hard work. "Some people make the mistake of thinking writing is an art," he observed. "It isn't. It is a craft that must be learned from the ground up and which can be perfected by working hard, day after day. It is simply a question of doing the job to the best of your ability" (Wharton). In recalling his early years of writing, he admitted that the forced routine was difficult: "But you've got to do it. . . . You know, it's not exactly a natural pursuit, a man putting himself in front of a typewriter—a machine—day after day. But you've got to spend three or four years digging yourself a rut so deep that finally you find it more convenient not to get out of it" (Fargo, 180–81).

In the early 1930s he was invited to teach a writing class at the University of Oregon and present a seminar at the University of Montana. He declined both invitations. He believed the writer's function in life is to write: "In ten years of writing I have gone ahead under the single conviction that nothing is of any importance except the actual fact of keeping on the job. My failures always have come when I forgot that and slacked off." He likened his temperament to that of "the old wheel-horse plodding down the road with always a load behind."[15] The work ethic developed in his youth, when he had to fend for himself, stayed with him. In refusing the teaching offer, he told Thacher in a letter, "I haven't yet shaken my freshman urge to smash through everything in the best 'bloody and unbowed' manner, I doubt if I ever do quite lose that inner attitude. I hope not."[16] "Bloody and unbowed" is of course an allusion to William Ernest Henley's "Invictus," a poem that meant much to him as he struggled to make a living in the early years of the depression. He spoke of it along with his belief in work in a 1931 letter to Arthur B. Epperson:

> I still cling to the old battle cry so beloved of my adolescence: life is real, life is earnest. And though I do not publish it for fear of universal ridicule I do believe most heartily, insofar as a personal working philosophy is concerned, the fine lines of Henley which have been so damned chawed up that they're now nothing but burlesque—beginning, "Out of the night that covers me, black as the pit from pole to pole." Distinctly do I believe that . . . the trouble with all of us is that we consider this life to be a pursuit of liberty and happiness. It's no such thing. When anybody starts pursuing happiness inevitably he'll wind up in the madhouse. Happiness is only and always a product of work well and faithfully done. No work—no happiness.[17]

Fortunately, he didn't permit this near obsession with work to isolate him from others. His rigorous writing routine was orderly enough to allow him to attend to his family; and he even deliberately sought civic service, which he thought would prevent the self-absorption writers are prone to.

Part of Haycox's attitude toward work was a conviction that any writer who becomes complacent about what he produces is headed downhill. He believed that the successful writer must remain a student, continually researching his subjects and enlarging and refining his techniques. Even within the firmly established conventions of the western, he said, "the thing to do is to study new ways of using old materials and reassembling them in such a way as to give the material vigor, vitality and color" (Wharton). He also suspected that worrying too much about literary success or feeling superior to the popular market could hinder the steady labor of improvement. When his editor at *Collier's* suggested that his 1935 story "High Wind" rivaled the fiction of Willa Cather, he replied with characteristic modesty that the compliment was kind, but dangerous to him:

> When any writer gets the hint that he may be writing near the edge of semi-permanent stuff a kind of malarial germ gets into his system. Every scribbler, I suppose, has buried in him the thought that someday he may turn out a spot of "deathless prose." It's a horrendous thing when it gets the upper hand, and fatal to good storytelling. When a man begins peeking over his shoulder at posterity all his writing muscles get a bad case of

cramps. The best job is always done on an ex tempore basis. In fact, I seem to have my most satisfactory days when I come to the office with a slight sinus attack and a knowledge that the rent is overdue. In this mood of low desperation I usually get something done.[18]

When Harold G. Merriam, a university professor educated at Oxford, Harvard, and Columbia universities, suggested that some of Haycox's short stories were too good for the market, Haycox thanked him but said it wasn't true: "Off-trail, maybe, or at odds with editorial policies. But a writer ought not make the mistake of shooting too far aside of his markets." The commercial market, he said, is wide and pretty catholic in taste: "If a man can't find somewhere a place for what he does he had better take another look at his story. The thing we must never forget is that we are writing to entertain people; that's our only business. If we cannot attract some sort of an audience what ground have we for saying our work is too good? A good job will always get applause. When a writer forgets that he is on the down grade."[19] These attitudes are modest, practical, and wise for a writer in his situation, but they may have contributed to his anguished postponement of divorcing himself from magazine publication. Eventually he recognized that the magazine market could not provide sufficient scope for his artistic ambitions.

Haycox's rigorous work ethic was part of his western populist conservatism. He believed there was no such thing as an Oregon writer, but there was such a thing as an Oregon temper: "For those who have lived here long and happily it is a definite thing compounded, among other elements, of about thirty per cent Puritan and five per cent hayseed. We cannot escape the effects of that blend, and for my part I would not want to."[20] His conservatism prevented him from being attracted by the literary-intellectual shift to the left during the 1930s. Instead, he remained a Republican and joined the Rotary Club. He had a tolerant appreciation of bohemianism and enjoyed Sinclair Lewis's satire of service clubs in *Babbitt,* but he was temperamentally inclined toward devotion to family, responsible citizenship, and optimism about American life. He could enjoy the company of Rotarians even while recognizing the pewter in them. He described his politics to Thacher in this way:

By chemical composition I'm a middle class fellow, believing in the capitalistic system, believing also in the primitive virtues, whatever they are. But I can't say that I'm attracted particularly to the well-to-do and socially proper and economically orthodox products of the system. They are a 65% dull lot. By profession I should be entirely with the innovators, experimenters and adventurous ones who claim they are leading the human spirit out of the morass. I think I should be for innovation if it weren't for the innovators. These blond Galahads of reform are as clever a set of people as ever rode a train on a government pass.

He distrusted "the intellectual with a Purpose" because such people are driven by a desire for power—"power of a central government, over the lives of people, and personal power for themselves as moving forces within that government." He thought such intellectual reformers are moved by "a definite antagonism of the old town meeting idea and a definite contempt for the idea that Si Punkinseed out in Corner Creek can govern himself."[21]

Social and political matters interested him greatly, and he expressed his opinions in letters to friends and in articles for *The Rotarian*. He opposed more government and less voice for the individual. He was critical of more taxes, welfare, unionization, radicalism, weakening of the judicial branch, and diminishing protection for minorities. He valued individual responsibility and discounted the idea that the state owes every person a living and a guarantee of security. He believed that freedom should be combined with discipline, a sense of obligation, and fidelity to principle and that these qualities should be fostered in the family. "It comes to me increasingly," he wrote Thacher in 1934, "that the one single, valid source of spiritual life now lies inside the home, particularly in the relation between parent and child."[22]

He was gloomy in enumerating what he considered to be alarming tendencies in American society, but he was not cynical. "There is apparently some chemical composition in me that makes enduring pessimism impossible," he told Thacher. "But I am rather indignant over the spectacle of a people that, having the greatest advantages and opportunities in the world, have gone soft and materialistic and pointless."[23] The burden of his essays in *The Rotarian* during the 1930s and 1940s was America's need for courage, resolution, and above all faith in itself. He knew that sociopolitical questions seldom have simple answers and that this fact leads people either to accept philosophies that pretend to have answers or to lapse into pessimism—"that pessimism which many of our 'best minds' accept." He favored instead a tough-minded process of coping with the complexity of human affairs.[24] Wallace Stegner's comment on writers reared in the West is particularly applicable to Haycox: "Any western writer may ultimately be grateful to his western upbringing for convincing him, beyond all chance of conversion, that man, even Modern Man, has some dignity if he will assume it, and that most lives are worth living even when they are lives of quiet desperation. The point is to do the best one can in the circumstances, not the worst."[25]

His essential optimism was also reflected in his literary tastes. Stories of bitterness and futility left him cold. He detected phoniness in them and suggested that they were often done for the same commercial reasons as the goriest pulp thriller. Sadness, he noted, is easy to make plausible in fiction; hope is not. And he didn't care for stories that are too thin a slice of life—"concerned with some microscopic section of human behavior expressed in some bizarre formula." He thought a story should be a full thing, "it should be a capsule-compressed collection of robust emotion and human interplay. Compression of a lot into a little—not a little into a lot." He liked Kipling and disliked Gertrude Stein. About the latter, he asked where's the beef: "Liverwurst appetizers tease the appetite, but it's the beef sandwich that nourishes the soul—if the beef's well cooked."[26]

How much of Haycox's life and opinions went into his fiction? That's difficult to determine. Formula fiction is not usually thought of as autobiographical; it seems to express conventions, not the author's personality. In fact the familiar conventions appear to offer an escape from both the author's and the reader's lives. But in a deeper sense, as Ross Macdonald has pointed out, the popular formula can provide the writer with "a mask for autobiography—a fencer's mask to deflect the cold steel of reality as he struggles with his own Falstaffian shadows. The convention provides means of disguising the authorial self, but that self reappears on other levels in the forms of other characters, and as the Hamlet's cloud on which the whole thing is projected."[27] Haycox's character and opinions are indeed discernible beneath the romance and action adventure of his fiction. The inner shape of his life, to borrow another analogy from Macdonald, supported his fiction like a skeleton, "just as intricate, almost as unchanging."[28]

Settling into the Slicks

The period from 1931 to 1935 was an important stage in Haycox's development. Appearing regularly in *Collier's* increased his confidence and intensified his persistent ambition to perfect his craft. For financial security, he continued writing for the pulps as well. Four of the five novels of this period were serialized in *Collier's*; the fifth appeared in *Short*

Stories, which had been the principal outlet for his fiction just prior to his recruitment by *Collier's*. He published 29 stories during this time in *Collier's* and 29 elsewhere, mostly in the pulps. This fiction, pulp and slick, is fairly uniform in quality, but the *Collier's* stories display greater divergence from the usual western formulas. He had been disappointed at first that writing for *Collier's* did not immediately allow him to escape formulaic conventions; but while he had to honor the magazine's policies, he refused simply to repeat himself. He experimented with vocabulary, dialogue, subject matter, psychological motivation, multiple plots, variety and multiplicity of characters, and ways of using mystery and suspense. He constantly tested the boundaries of editorial policy. That policy was more flexible regarding short stories than it was when featured serials were concerned, but he forced the issue with two of the five serialized novels of this period.

The five novels were *Starlight Rider* (1933), *Riders West* (1934), *Rough Air* (1934), *The Silver Desert* (1935), and *Trail Smoke* (1935). Three of these are conventional westerns; *Rough Air* and *The Silver Desert* are not. *Rough Air* is about aviation and Hollywood, two subjects in vogue in the magazine market at the time. *The Silver Desert* is the usual sort of ranch conflict, but with two significant variations: it is set in the present and includes a group of characters from Hollywood. The heroine, in fact, is a film actress on the threshold of stardom. Some of the short stories go even further in diverging from standard horse opera. A number of them have contemporary settings and include such ingredients as aviation, Hollywood, and rodeoing. Even those set in the late nineteenth century often are devoid of the usual chases and showdowns. The settings are western, but the conflicts are often moral and psychological rather than physical.

Haycox's immediate concern during the early 1930s was to entertain his audience and thereby make a living, but he was not the sort of person who could engage in that project without bringing his social and moral concerns to bear upon it. Besides selling stories, he was selling his version of a western way of life. When he set his stories in contemporary Pendleton, Reno, or Hollywood, his underlying intention was to explore the extent to which frontier values and mores have persisted into the present and the extent to which they have been altered by collectivism, materialism, and shallow sophistication. When he set his stories in late-nineteenth-century Nebraska, he explored retrospectively the strengths and weaknesses of frontier society. Haycox the commercial writer was oriented by Haycox the social historian: his entertainment fiction was shaped by serious sociohistorical interests and firm moral commitments. In writing about the West, he recognized a need for a continuity between the past and present, a need commonly ignored by writers of westerns, most of whom write only of the past. He practiced the advice Wallace Stegner later provided to westerners who write about the West: "We must not choose between the past and present but instead try to find connections between them, try to make one serve the other" (Stegner, 200–201).

Rough Air is the story of a former World War I flyer, Jim, who now works in Hollywood as a stunt pilot. He doesn't fit in Hollywood and feels like a relic of an earlier time of flying adventure. Flying has become a business. The pioneering is over: the oceans have been flown and the trade lanes charted. Particularly when he is in the air, he knows he belongs to a simpler time when independence and purposeful courage mattered. In Hollywood, the narrator tells us, "nobody knew anything, nobody was sure, nobody was happy. Nothing was certain but a kind of cannibalistic ambition that drove the unknown and scourged the great. . . . Show people—walking the quicksands of lucky breaks, and favor from high places, and fickle public taste. It was all very bright and fine, like the camera side of a scene; but on the other side was the flimsy falsework supporting the illusion." The heroine, Anne, is also out of place in Hollywood. She is from the Oregon desert, "where you have to possess hope—and a lot of patience." She loves that country and "could go back and live in a tar-paper shanty and tend irrigation ditches and ride fence—and be well content." And in fact she and Jim eventually do return to Oregon, where the opening scene of the novel was set. At the end, atop an Oregon hill, Anne says to Jim, "You and I—we were never meant to live in a world as fast and skeptical and worldly wise as the one in Hollywood. It was bad medicine." Jim replies, "No. You can see a lot of things from this hillside, Anne." They cling to each other there "like two children rejoined after a long separation in the dark."

This attachment to Oregon—to the West—is not a mere device in Haycox's fiction; it was deeply felt. A transparently autobiographical story published the same year as *Rough Air* makes this clear.[29] A writer and his wife return from Portland to New York City after 10 years. Both native westerners, they had met and married and been poor in the city and had vowed to return when they could stay at the Plaza and shop in the best stores. But they are not happy with their return—something is wrong. They understand their disappointment when they see an Albert Bierstadt painting in a window, an enormous Rocky Mountain scene:

"These two people were Western purely, and that painting was like a call across the continent." This couple—a fictional version of Erny and Jill—are firmly rooted in the West, and, as Haycox once told his editor, "I do not transplant well."[30]

Rough Air was an interesting experiment, but less than successful. The flying fails to accomplish what Haycox was able to do with the western formulas. The novel includes a California murder mystery with a Hammett-Chandler flavor. The dialogue is brisk and sophisticated—very different from the rural vernacular frequent in his westerns. These things indicate the versatility of Haycox's imagination and technique, but the novel is weakened by the hero's being out of his element. Jim would like to act and combat "the evil net surrounding Anne Carson, yet however he might approach the problem Hollywood stood in his way—its subtle and ironically civilized forms taunting his helplessness." The novel conveys in sharp relief the contrast that preoccupied Haycox—between frontier and modern urban values, between West and East (Hollywood being part of the East despite geographical location)—but the hero is handicapped by an environment in which physical strength and self-reliant integrity are of little avail.

This weakness is remedied in *The Silver Desert*. The action again occurs in the early 1930s, but this time the Hollywood people come to a Nevada ranch. There the hero, a rancher protecting his property from land grabbers, can demonstrate the usual frontier strengths within a conventional western plot. In visiting Nevada about this time, Haycox had been struck by the juxtaposition of old and new: "Nevada is one of the states in the West in which you will find striking combinations of the frontier atmosphere and the ultra-smart modern atmosphere. In Reno you find the meeting place of all these elements—the wealthy seekers after divorce, people from the East and from Hollywood. Piute Indians, cowboys, ranchers, prospectors. You'll run into all of them in a walk down the street. . . . Up in the North, toward the Oregon line, you still find cattle country not much changed from the character it had in the old days."[31] This seemed the perfect setting for exploring the persistence of the old ways and their confrontation with the new. But *Collier's* was skeptical and rejected the novel at first on the grounds that the action was laid too implausibly close to Reno. "I wish I could get those fellows to see what the country forty miles from Reno looks like!" Haycox complained to Thacher.[32] After some revision *Collier's* relented. In the final version the ranch is described as being 140 miles and 60 years from Reno.

The question as to how much of the Old West has survived is explicitly aired at the beginning in a conversation between the Hollywood people and the Nevadans. There are jokes about all the rustlers and robbers now being in Hollywood making movies. Tom, the rancher hero, says to Lily, the actress heroine, "You don't have much faith in the traditional West, do you?" She replies, "I think you cling to sentimental memories. You are a modern man, but you wish to believe you are part of the old times." One of the old-timers good naturedly charges the young Hollywood set with lacking belief in anything: "You people forbid yourselves the luxury of honest emotion because you're afraid of it. So you are all turning brittle and transparent." All this conversation has specific relevance to Lily, who has come to Reno because she suspects the stardom awaiting her: she craves "the real," a purpose in life she can respect. And of course by the end she has found it in the rather anachronistic ranch conflict and the courage, integrity, and self-reliance demonstrated by the hero. Haycox's premise is that frontier values are alive and relevant; they are not, as Lily imagines in the beginning, "the crinoline and linsey woolsey of a dead age" tucked away in an attic trunk.

The novel has a number of strengths: tense action, interesting subplots, psychological depth, and intriguing secrets regarding father-son relationships. But having such riding and shooting take place in the 1930s tests the reader's sense of plausibility. Moreover, the blending of cowboy conflict and Hollywood is imperfect: the Hollywood people, merely guests at the ranch, are uninvolved in the action and scarcely know what is going on. Their superficiality simply enhances by contrast the western values the author wishes to promote.

A more penetrating examination of frontier life is provided by a cluster of five short stories Haycox wrote for *Collier's* during this time.[33] These stories are about the community of New Hope, Nebraska, in the late nineteenth century, and it is the community itself—its social and moral character—that is the real subject. Reflections on frontier history rather than narratives of action adventure, these stories display considerable literary excellence and artistic seriousness. Four of them are told from the first-person point of view, a technique Haycox had seldom used before. The narrator, in his sixties, remembers incidents from his childhood, incidents he observed from a child's perspective but now understands through the wisdom of age. These are stories of initiation into experience within the context of a transitional stage in frontier life; they both celebrate and criticize a particular time and place and thereby illuminate an era of our national history. They reveal a part of Haycox's talent that was perhaps never fully displayed in his novels. His keen interest in history—not so much in stirring events as in ordinary lives, in customs, attitudes, and social behavior—is clearly apparent. His power of reflection, which had to be restrained from inhibiting the pace of action in his adventure novels, is given freer rein.

Haycox selected the setting strategically, not simply as background for the action but because it was inherently interesting to him. New Hope represents a significant time and place in the settlement of the West. The town is established enough to have schools and churches and its own gentility, but it still exists on the edge of violence and insecurity: "South of us in Kansas and Missouri the bandit gangs still scourged the country and the border ruffianism of the war still smoldered. West of us lay the great prairie reaching out its trackless distances; a hundred and fifty miles that way the cattle trails and the trail towns still roared. We could not escape that raw world."[34] In this community, the coarse and transient exist alongside the respectable and established; this makes the latter self-conscious and defensive of their hard-earned respectability and therefore narrow-minded and class-conscious. They are strong and essentially good people but cruel in their volatile intolerance: "They had to be a dogged, hard-fibered sort to absorb the shocks of a raw land. But, tied into monotony and the grinding work of the day, there was in them a deep appetite for relief, and relief came to them only in vivid, violent emotional outbursts: the election campaign, the murder trial, or the revival meeting that gave them their only relaxation from the discipline of the frontier."[35] The conformist moral and social standards, the class snobbery, derive largely from a fear of this latent violence. These stories are perceptive case studies of community psychology, products of a skilled social historian rather than a horse-opera hack.

On the one hand, these stories nostalgically evoke the atmosphere of the town and the era. Haycox is adroit at such description, skillfully blending research and imagination to capture the positive qualities of both the physical and social environment. On the other hand, they are a probing indictment of self-righteous intolerance, which, at this stage in the evolution of the frontier, existed concomitantly with those admirable virtues that made a prosperous community possible. Bigoted ostracism and persecution are threads woven into each of the stories, and Haycox implies that these threads continue in the fabric of American society. When the narrator of "Their Own Lights" describes a public hanging as "the flaming cross of an outraged justice," Haycox is evoking the specter of Ku Klux Klan activities in his own time. The violence in the cause of right that Haycox glorified in his action serials received closer scrutiny in these vignettes of frontier society.

Besides its preoccupation with the western American way of life, Haycox's fiction of the early 1930s is also important for its development of the rather melancholy, fatalistic hero. This hero has been likened to Hamlet and is considered one of the author's principal contributions to the genre. The type emerged in its full form in the novels of this period. The heroes are individualized enough to be distinct and interesting, but, for the sake of generalization, they can fairly be characterized as a single hero. This is a man who believes the bewildering book of destiny is already written: nothing changes, and there are no answers to the big questions: "There was a pattern to a man's life and it never changed; there was a fate that covered him from beginning to end and neither hope nor bitter fighting could temper that" (*Trail Smoke*). The hero tells us, "I've had a lot knocked out of me, and some pretty hard wisdom driven into me." The only sure fact for him is that "the dark gods attending his destiny looked on now and cared not at all. . . . There was no end, no promise of eventual tranquility or profit." "Restless, skeptical, perplexed by a world in which he saw no plan, he clung the more rigidly to those few convictions he had" (*Starlight Rider*). He tells his young companion, "The morning half of a trail is always fresh and full of new things, kid. But the afternoon half is a tedious journey, for there's nothing on it you haven't seen before." He has missed most of the joy of life: "There was a melody in the world, for he had heard it, and there was some meaning for men in the world, for he had seen other men's faces light up on discovering it. Neither was for him; vaguely, as a traveler on a lonely trail, he had seen the lamp-glow of hope far away—and then had passed on." When the heroine asks him about his sadness, he answers, "I want something I can't have" (*Trail Smoke*) or "I should like to believe in many good things and can't see my way clear to do it" (*Starlight Rider*). In a violent world the good man is forced to kill in order to maintain a shred of justice and meaning, but in killing he becomes like the evil man, and this weighs upon his conscience. In short, behind the fast-paced action of these novels is a crisis of belief, of faith in a meaningful world—a tension between free will and determinism.

This tension provides a kind of tragic dimension. Popular romantic adventure is of course no place for the tragic: it is the realm of melodrama. Nevertheless, a tincture of the tragic does add verisimilitude and a certain depth; it makes the characters more plausible and psychologically interesting. And of course the fatalistic brooding, the crisis of belief, is

not left unresolved. The hero continues to act with purpose despite his
fatalism. When the heroine accuses him of fatalism, he counters, "I'm a
fatalist only as to the setup and eventual ending. I admit the rules of the
game can't be changed. But inside those rules I do what I please. It is up
to me to survive or die" (*The Silver Desert*). When his companion questions the meaning of life by asking, "Well, what in thunder is it all about
then?" the hero replies, "There is no answer," and then immediately
adds, "But if a man was meant for anything, I guess it is to keep ram-
ming ahead till he finds something that will do for an answer." His companion chides him for the way he puzzles over the big questions and
meanwhile continues to act: "Your old thinker don't track with your
muscles" (*Starlight Rider*). This, in a nutshell, is the characteristic Haycox
hero: a man acting purposefully in an apparently purposeless world, a
melancholy man who cannot bear to see others made unhappy.

By the end of each story the hero does indeed find something that
will do for an answer: the woman who gives life meaning and quiets his
restless discontent. And finding the women always corresponds with an
end of the cycle of violence. The fatalism has served as a skillful device
for generating tension and suspense, a complement to the suspense created by the physical conflict. This was a significant and much-imitated
addition to the western formula. But it was not merely a device, a commercial gimmick. Haycox's inner life involved a dialectic of freedom and
determinism, of idealism and naturalism. Like the shuttlecock in a bad-
minton game, his attitude was impelled alternately by the rackets of
naive optimism and cynical despair. He was a romantic with an ineradi-
cable strain of optimism in his temperament, yet his vision of life had a
naturalistic cast.

Augmenting the fatalism in these novels is a distinctive treatment of
western landscape. The beauty and spaciousness of the natural world,
particularly at night, both prompt the deep questions and, at the same
time, hint at answers. Sometimes nature speaks mystery: "Out of the
hills—out of the far sweep of canyon and ridge and of pine-deep—
prowled the ghostly, abysmal feel of loneliness, of mystery primitive and
unsolvable. This was night, with night's riddle walking on his nerves. It
was, [he] thought, the cold touch of a nameless and timeless question,
reaching out of a black sky into a man's heart." At other times nature
speaks comfort: "All the details of this mountain world were vivid and
pleasant. They fed his senses in a way that was strange to him, fulfilling
a hunger he did not understand, covering him with a comfort and a
familiarity." As the hero rolls up in his blanket near the campfire, "Out

of this deep solitude came the air-borne call of wildness, intangible, yet striking definitely through him." The tightness and bitterness drain from him, and he smiles, even chuckles to himself, as he goes to sleep, "the presence of that wild mystery invoking a swift response in his wire-tough body. It eased and nourished him, though he did not know why. There was some ancient familiarity here he didn't understand" (*Trail Smoke*). While the hero might feel that his life is full of dark alleys blind at the ending, he nevertheless experiences moments outdoors "when all the pagan splendors of the raw land stirred in him an ancient, primeval response. Such things as the crystal pathway of stars stretching across infinity, the sweep of Powder Desert all golden in the morning, or some feeling of supreme fitness and unity that passed before the glow of it was quite established" (*Starlight Rider*).

Haycox clearly understood that the popular western must involve the reader with a strong sense of locale. The genre, after all, is named for a geographical location and is above all about a place. The narrative must be characteristic of the West and the setting itself a generating force, not merely a backdrop for action that could have occurred somewhere else. For this to happen successfully, a sympathetic understanding based on knowledge and feeling of the land's features—both animate and inanimate—is necessary. "I feel this West distinctly," Haycox said. "The romance has perhaps been overplayed and now and then the grim brutality has been overplayed. But there she lies, with ten thousand stories not yet told."[36] He had respect for nature rather than romantic love for it—or at least his respect ran deeper than his love. Nature's primordial variety includes beauties that are easy to love and a vastness that prompts reverential wonder, but it also includes, as Haycox well knew, an indifferent and implacable force that can suddenly or gradually destroy a human life. And the western landscape could also contribute to the characteristic melancholy of the Haycox hero. A Texas rancher once observed that "the cowboy of the West worked in a land that seemed to be grieving over something—a kind of sadness, loneliness in a deathly quiet. One not acquainted with the plains could not understand what effect it had on the mind. It produced a heartache and a sense of exile."[37] Haycox, intimately familiar with western landscape, understood this effect on the mind: "The land lay locked in a silence and a mystery so deeply felt by riders of the range that in time it became a part of them, flavoring their talk, influencing their acts" ("Return of a Fighter").

Haycox's fiction from 1931 to 1935 displays both a repetition of formulas and a remarkably imaginative effort to vary and enlarge them.

The western ethos was his paramount interest: its codes of behavior, its differences from the ethos of the East, its tensions between individual and community, its manifestation in women as well as men; its persistence into the twentieth century. From his treatment of this ethos emerged a slightly melancholy and fatalistic hero who finds contentment by the end of each story in the right woman and a piece of land. The contentment is earned by courage and integrity in a fight against greed and injustice. This pattern is enacted in a western landscape, vividly described, symbolically resonant, and vitally conducive to the western ethos.

This fiction also reveals Haycox's increasing predilection for history, manifest not by treating specific historical people or events but rather by treating the customs and mores of western life. His attention to the role of women and the nature of gender conflicts on the frontier is part of this historical orientation, as is his expanding variety of character types, providing a cross-section of western society.

Collier's published *The Silver Desert* with some qualms and insisted that Haycox follow it with a more conventional western. This he did in *Trail Smoke*, a fine formula western that can be viewed as the culmination of this stage of his career. It has a large cast of characters, many of whom are psychologically interesting and plausible. The hero combines intelligence and self-reflection with physical strength. The action is fluently plotted and heightened with mystery and suspense. Multiple strands of narrative are woven into an organic whole. The author's characteristic two-women motif is skillfully used and creates an engaging and suspenseful love interest. Things are subtly communicated between characters without being said, thus providing both economy and suggestiveness. The physical action is complemented by psychological tensions in family relationships. In short, *Trail Smoke* is the category western at its best and displays Haycox's mastery of the genre. From this point on he would repeat that mastery while at the same time wrestling with his ambition to go beyond it. And the avenue leading beyond seemed to him to be the historical novel.

Chapter Four

From Horse Opera to History

Featured in *Collier's*

From 1936 to 1942 Haycox's fiction first appeared exclusively in *Collier's*. His agent, Sydney A. Sanders, was free to submit the stories anywhere, and occasionally he tried other magazines, but, as things turned out, everything appeared first in *Collier's*. The novels, after serialization, were then published as books. This connection with a single magazine was a mutually satisfactory situation: Haycox was pleased to be reaching a large audience, making a good living, and having a certain latitude for artistic growth; and the magazine's editors were pleased to be publishing the writer they considered the best in the field. By an agreement established in 1936, Haycox received $15,000 for serials written in about 10 installments of approximately 7,500 words. By 1938 Sanders was asking for an increase.[1] Each short story was earning at this time at least $800.[2]

William L. Chenery, the general editor of *Collier's*, admired the stories and serials so much that, after a business trip to San Francisco in January 1937, he made a special visit to Haycox in Portland. In March of the same year he wrote to Haycox, "It seems to me that your work is improving steadily and I take great pleasure in that. You have a real gift for narrative and I think that your character work is getting richer as you move along. I hope that you continue to give your best to your writing and I am certain that if you continue to grow as you have in the last few years, the future will be very bright for you and your charming family."[3] Some months later he wrote with praise for "A Day in Town," a story of a homesteader whose strength of character alone is enough for a banker to grant him a loan: "As you know I like most of your short stories but this one strikes me as being particularly fresh and moving. You have managed to avoid a few phrases that you were beginning to like and that, too, is good. I am glad to see you develop and do better work as time passes on. . . . [Y]ou are unquestionably growing and not everybody is able to do better work as he becomes successful."[4] This was satisfying

praise coming from one of the country's distinguished editors and a man
Haycox highly respected. He had a photograph of Chenery on his wall
and mentioned to him, "I do not know if you consider the company
quite respectable or not, but you hang on the office wall between Calvin
Coolidge and an old-time pioneer of Eastern Oregon who killed two
white men and several Indians."[5]

His relationship with *Collier's* fiction editor, Kenneth Littauer, was
equally cordial. They exchanged letters, visits, and gifts. Occasionally,
Littauer would wire that he needed a story badly, and Haycox would
reliably provide it. In 1937 Littauer wrote, "We have never had to buy a
bad story from you. And since your work continues to improve and to
mature from year to year it is unlikely that we shall ever have to."[6]

Letters to *Collier's* from Haycox and Sanders occasionally express
appreciation for acceptance of stories diverging from presumed market
needs. Haycox was continually testing the boundaries of editorial policy,
and not every story was accepted, although rejection was rare. In 1939
Littauer wrote to Sanders, "Here is a story by Ernest Haycox called
BOYHOOD which neither COLLIER'S nor the COMPANION wants
to buy. This is a red letter day in the history of the publishing business.
Literary chronicalists for centuries will be referring to it as the great
Haycox crisis."[7] Praise and encouragement from his editors came in tan-
dem with such occasional rejections and reminders that formula action
adventure was what they really wanted from him. These mixed signals
increased the vacillation of purpose already apparent in his writing. The
novels and stories of this period alternate between formula cowboy stories and narratives of frontier history and character, with an occasional
contemporary romance added to the bargain.[8]

Haycox's first historical western, *Trouble Shooter*, was serialized in
1936. He had been interested in American history from the beginning of
his career, as the many history books in his library and the Revolutionary
War stories he wrote in the 1920s make clear. But *Trouble Shooter* was his
first attempt to base a novel on an actual event and include historical
characters. Why hadn't he done this before? One would expect that an
audience who liked westerns would be especially interested in western
history, but the fact is that the audience for pulp westerns during the
1920s and 1930s was much more interested in action and romance. For
example, when Harold B. Hersey launched *Ace-High* he thought the
public would go for a little education along with entertainment, but he
was soon disillusioned. He ran a series of historical articles called "The
Making of America, State by State," but he found that readers would

only buy formula westerns. He concluded that he must simply entertain, and he never again deviated from that principle.[9] Haycox, who knew market tastes as well as anyone, understood that shifting from romantic adventure to history was risky. Consequently, he made the shift gradually and tentatively.

Trouble Shooter is dedicated to Thacher, which suggests that Haycox had aimed for something he thought his teacher and literary conscience would appreciate. In its conception, the novel moves toward the ideal Haycox thought best suited to his interests and talents: the panoramic historical novel with multiple characters and plot lines and plenty of action and emotion. His preliminary synopsis for his editors emphasizes the dramatic historical context for the action: the building of the Union Pacific Railroad from Cheyenne to Promontory Point during 1868–69. A sheet of notes titled "Main Threads" lists 10 items of plot and subplots. A sheet titled "Characters" lists three groups: five main characters, 15 secondary, and five historical. The historical characters are President Grant and four men responsible for the project: General Grenville Dodge, Samuel Reed, and Daniel and Jack Casement. These figures are incidental to the main action, which involves the characteristic Haycox hero and close companions, two heroines, and assorted villains. Edwin L. Sabin's *Building the Pacific Railway* was the principal source, but Haycox's personal library includes annotated copies of J. R. Perkins's *Trails, Rails, and War*, a biography of Dodge; Dodge's *How We Built the Union Pacific*; Nelson Trottman's *History of the Union Pacific*; and pamphlets issued by the Union Pacific during the building of the railway. Haycox's research notes include information on such things as surveying, coal, timber, railroad personnel, tables of distances, chronologies, descriptions of the work, sources of financing, and Indians. In addition to reading, he traveled the route to absorb images of the landscape. All this amounted to considerable research, but none of it is obtrusive in the narrative; Haycox, trained in the entertainment market of the pulps, knew that engaging action and emotion must take precedence over historical facts no matter how interesting or authentic.

The role of historical authenticity in westerns is an important and debated theoretical issue and particularly relevant in the case of Haycox. Bernard DeVoto, an early and influential critic of the genre, insisted that historical accuracy was of first importance. Primarily a historian, he valued facts and reality over myth and romance.[10] In the 1950s he would single out Haycox as the writer who came closest to making good literature out of the western myths, but at the time *Trouble Shooter* appeared he was unimpressed with Haycox's treatment of history. In a *Saturday Review* editorial for 24 April 1937, DeVoto, in his own inimitable way, pronounced upon the subject of western fiction, discounting the suggestion that a new fashion of deeper and more intelligent cattle-kingdom westerns was possible: "Thirty years of cheap fiction about cowboys, rustlers, evil sheriffs, roundups, stampedes, six-guns, and branding irons have created an inertia which serious literature finds it hard to overcome." He suggested that writers would have to abandon the cattle kingdom and move "farther back and farther West, before 1860 and beyond the hundredth meridian," in order to create good fiction. He pointed out that the western migration had rich literary potential that remained untapped and merited better treatment than it had received. He mentioned in particular that the transcontinental railroad building deserved better than Zane Grey's "preposterous *U.P. Trail* and a sentimental romance in *Collier's*." The historical fiction he envisioned would be "realistic, hard-bitten, and unrhetorical."[11]

The "romance" alluded to is *Trouble Shooter*. Sanders, Haycox's literary agent, spotted the editorial and sent it to Haycox, who responded in a letter that Sanders shared with Littauer, who in turn passed it on to Chenery. The keen interest of author, agent, and editors in an offhand allusion by DeVoto is revealing in several ways. It indicates that when DeVoto spoke of western fiction, those who wrote and published it listened. Westerns were an important part of *Collier's* literary offerings at the time, and Haycox was a highly prized regular. Author, agent, and editors were also alert to DeVoto's views on the possibility of quality westerns because they were ambivalent about that possibility themselves. Haycox desired to write serious novels about the West but was locked into the lucrative magazine market and was struggling to determine how much literary sophistication that market would bear. His agent and editors knew how good a writer he was and sympathized with his literary ambitions, and sometimes encouraged them, but ultimately they heeded the market. They were in the anomalous position of being offended by DeVoto's calling Haycox's novel a "sentimental romance" and at the same time responsible for bridling him to magazine market expectations.

In a letter to Sanders, Haycox responded to the editorial with some disagreement, but also with a considerable amount of assent. DeVoto's views pricked his deepest concerns as a writer and prompted him to articulate them. Even though stung by DeVoto's downgrading of westerns and particularly by the specific reference to his own novel, he graciously acknowledged, "I'll go along with much that he says." He even modestly conceded that his railroad novel was sentimental: "I can see passages of that as clearly as he can." But he thought DeVoto put too much emphasis on a fiction that must be "realistic, hard-bitten, and unrhetorical." He saw that emphasis as merely a vogue of the time. This was 1937, when literary fashion leaned toward sociopolitical statement. Haycox did not propose "to make the mistake of writing any Purposeful fiction with 'sociological implications' as DeVoto seems to consider the prime function of fiction." He thought such contemporary fiction ignored important aspects of human experience and sentiment:

> Trouble with so many of these tea-tasters of fiction is that they think writing should be a gal who wears a smock, bobs her hair and is wedded (in the eyes of God at least) to a Cause. Which is wrong. A good story may draw many pictures and leave many inferences, but its prime purpose is to be a good story, with live people. We are all straining too hard for the Golden Apple. We are all spreading our talents too thin. And most of us are touched by the modern curse—afraid of broad humanity in our stories. The women of the old painters were ample, buxom and vital. The modern ones are raised on lettuce leaves. So it is with stories. Oh well.

As this passage indicates, Haycox in his letters was a pretty good match for DeVoto at turning a phrase. There may be a question about his reading of what DeVoto meant by "realistic, hard-bitten, and unrhetorical," but the important thing is that DeVoto's editorial prompted him to express what was weighing on his mind at the time and increasingly until his death: the ambition to write serious historical novels about the West. "The trouble with most writers, including me," he remarked in the same letter, "is that they thresh around, seeking a medium of expression and a field. I have the field but not the medium."[12] His field was the American West; his problem with medium was making the choice between magazine serial and serious novel. He was expert at the former but unsure of himself in attempting the latter. Because of temperament and writing experience, he respected the subject of romantic adventure; but literary fashion, as expressed by DeVoto, seemed to dictate that romantic adventure was out of bounds for a first-rate author.

DeVoto's views on westerns and the possibilities of realistic treatment of a broader range of western experiences naturally riveted Haycox's attention. His short stories were already oriented away from the stock properties of category westerns and continued in that direction until his death. Changing the orientation of his novels was more problematic: they were so popular that his editors wanted no deviation from successful patterns. Eventually, after much artistic anxiety and effort, he divorced himself from magazine publication and devoted himself to narratives about Oregon history. Thus, although he quibbled with DeVoto's pronouncements, he in fact followed in his subsequent career the course indicated by the editorial: a moving back before 1860, an abandonment of the cattle kingdom with its myths and conventions, a treatment of pioneering in the far West, and a more realistic, even naturalistic depiction of human behavior.

Chenery was delighted to learn that Haycox was "not going to make the mistake of writing any Purposeful fiction with 'sociological implications.'" This seems a peculiar comment from an editor, but it must be seen in context. Chenery wasn't hostile to sociological implications; he simply meant that they were not useful when deliberately contrived in art and literature: "I think that if you tell the best and truest stories you can find of the West, you won't have to worry about sociology or implications."[13] The real point here in connection with DeVoto's theory and Haycox's practice is whether in fact it was possible to "tell the best and truest stories" of the West within the popular magazine medium using the conventions of cowboy fiction. Haycox, apparently confirming DeVoto's assertions, ultimately felt it was not.

Following *Trouble Shooter*, Haycox turned away from the overtly historical western and produced three cowboy serials: *Deep West* (1937), *Sundown Jim* (1937), and *Man in the Saddle* (1938). With *Deep West* he changed his hardcover publisher from Doubleday to Little, Brown. This was a good decision because Little, Brown was a more respected firm, willing to provide the increased advertising that produced greater sales. These three novels were fine additions to the cowboy genre. They are peopled with numerous and varied characters; the familiar plots resonate afresh with the particular detail and intriguing twists of a first-rate imagination; the women are distinctive personalities who interest the reader as well as the hero; and the villains vary greatly in age, physical stature, and psychological motivation. These novels retain the essential patterns that draw readers to popular fiction, but they thicken the texture of setting, characterization, and motivation. Other writers recognized the quality of Haycox's imagination and the freshness of his techniques and benefited from his models.

At the same time Haycox was producing these action serials, he was questioning himself about the possibilities of his talent and planning more challenging and significant projects. A letter to Thacher early in 1938 reveals his preoccupations.[14] He had naturally fretted over the question, "Would a man, coming up to a writing career through the pulp route, damn and dim his spiritual unmentionables to the extent that he could do nothing better?" This is the main question of his career, and in his case an untimely death left it for the most part unanswered. But his answer in 1938 was that it depends on the man: "1. how great an imaginative equipment he had to begin with, 2. how capable he is of growth in the matter of understanding and perception, 3. how his brute energy holds out." His confidence that he was the right kind of man is unstated but strongly implied. He went on to say that he lacked the answer for the next question: "Where do I go from here?" For 15 years he had been learning to write, and technically he knew how. The next step was to find "a field or a subject or a period or a set of characters" that would allow him to use all that he knew and felt and thus determine whether he was "one of the angels or one of the kitchen help." His plan at this time was for a large historical novel set in Arizona from 1865 to 1885 that would cover the period from emptiness to civilization, from Apache wars through the founding of ranches and towns: "Partly it is pioneering, partly a frontier reflection on America's General Grant era in political and economic morals, partly it is the strange overlay of romanticism on a most primitive kind of social morals; chiefly it is people."

This ambitious plan reveals Haycox's interests and aspirations, but it was unrealistic within the context of his present writing situation. Such a project would require considerable time to research and write. Meanwhile, *Collier's* expected from him a regular and predictable flow of conventional western serials. Moreover, it is unlikely that the magazine would have been interested in a large historical novel that failed to conform to its requirements for length and audience appeal. And Haycox, at the top of the serial market, was not prepared to break from it. His next novel, *The Border Trumpet* (1939), is a compromise between these literary and practical considerations. It is set in Arizona during the early 1870s, and the historical background and geographical details are accurate, drawn mostly from John G. Bourke's *On the Border with Crook*. But it spans just a few months of time and focuses on military life and fighting with Apaches at the frontier station of Fort Grant. Love and adventure take precedence over history in a blending of fiction and history that pleased readers. This was Haycox's first cavalry novel. He had warmed up with the subject in short stories, and more military narratives would follow, including one of his best-known novels, *Bugles in the Afternoon*.

The subject was congenial to his interest in male comradeship, courage, duty, and codes of conduct.

Despite the success of *The Border Trumpet*, Haycox turned aside again from the historical western to write three more cowboy novels: *Saddle and Ride* (1939–40), *Rim of the Desert* (1940), and *Trail Town* (1941). The latter is generally patterned after Marshall Tom Smith's tough control of Abilene, but none of these narratives is historical in a strict sense. Haycox had plenty of ideas for historical novels and mentioned them to Littauer. The subjects included Aaron Burr, Andrew Jackson, the Mexican Way, Kansas in the 1850s, and homesteading in Nebraska. Littauer was only lukewarm about the suggestions, fearing that history would get in the way of romance.[15] Chenery also discouraged him from more than infrequent historical narratives. It was not until *Alder Gulch* (1941–42) that he again turned to specific historical events and people. The events were the discovery of gold at Alder Gulch, Montana, in 1864 and the vigilante action spawned by the accompanying lawlessness. The people include Henry Plummer, the corrupt sheriff masterminding the outlaws. But the fictional characters are the center of interest: a hero who has retreated into detached individualism because of painful experiences in childhood and in the Civil War, and a heroine who thirsts for adventure and flees to the gold camp to avoid marrying a dull man she doesn't love. The moral struggle between individualism and responsibility to community, which fascinated Haycox, is treated here with depth and skill, and the romance and action are complemented by an accurately detailed historical background. Haycox was mastering the possibilities of the historical western, but he still felt obliged (by considerations of money, guaranteed success, and requests from agent and editors) to continue producing conventional cowboy narratives. His next two novels, *Action by Night* (1942) and *The Wild Bunch* (1943), fall into that category. They are competent westerns—Haycox's fiction never fluctuated significantly in the quality of its technique—but they lack the richness of *Alder Gulch*.

The short stories of this period (1936–42) are too numerous and diverse for specific consideration in this brief study. Some of them, although technically competent, are of slight depth and merely reflect the tastes of magazine readers of the time; others, however, are of excellent quality and merit careful literary evaluation. Haycox excelled in compression. He was adroit at delineating character with brief but telling description and richly nuanced dialogue. There are no wasted events: each action resonates with implications for character and theme.

A good example of these qualities is "Stage to Lordsburg" (10 April 1937), on which John Ford's famous film *Stagecoach* (1939) was based. Into this story of about 14 pages is compressed enough variety in people, emotion, and event for a substantial novel, yet the story is satisfyingly complete in itself.

As diverse as the stories are, they all treat in some way the history and ethos of the American West. For example, there are two miniature sagas of strong, ambitious cattlemen who succeed in wealth and power but fail in love and family. A number of stories examine homesteading and portray the kinds of populist values Haycox admired: working one's own land, neighborliness, personal integrity, family unity, endurance, common sense over sophisticated learning, personal freedom for oneself and others. One story is a somber, unromantic portrayal of marriage between a white man and an Indian woman. Several military stories have little action and no young love interest; instead, they examine the personal costs of duty and leadership or being an army wife on the frontier. In short, many of the stories of this period explore with perceptive seriousness and literary artistry the problematic aspects of frontier life that in the novels are overshadowed by romance and adventure. *Collier's* sometimes published them reluctantly for the sake of humoring their master supplier of action romance. Haycox's achievement as an author of short fiction deserves recognition alongside his success as a novelist. It is an achievement largely outside the myths and formulas of the category western.

History and Fiction

Haycox gravitated toward the historical western for several reasons. As mentioned, he had an early and abiding interest in American history and found pleasure in historical research, particularly in visiting sites, examining remnants of material culture, and reading firsthand accounts of frontier life. And this interest complemented his literary ambitions because the historical western is the most literary version of the conventional western adventure story. Historical accuracy not only lent more realism and credibility to his stories, but it also allowed him to explore the western ethos in more than vague mythic terms. Moreover—canny professional that he was—Haycox sensed the enthusiasm for historical fiction emerging in the 1930s and 1940s. As James D. Hart explains in *The Popular Book: A History of America's Literary Taste*, this was a period of special popularity for historical fiction: "A period of stress and turmoil, leading people to books both for escape and explanation, favored the revival of historical novels. In a time when to face the present or the future was unpleasant, looking backward was a comparative pleasure, affording surcease from contemporary problems and an understanding that people of other ages had weathered worse times."[16]

Visiting the pressroom at the Portland police headquarters nearly 20 years after he worked there as a reporter, Haycox said, "I learned one lesson in this press room that has stood me in good stead ever since. I learned the importance of accuracy. And accuracy is the keystone of fiction writing. . . . [W]hen I make an error I am deluged with letters of complaint from magazine readers all over the country."[17] Elsewhere he mentioned having once started the sagebrush 100 miles too far east in Nebraska, and "they formed clubs back there" to write and tell him about it (Haycox, Jr., vii). In regard to *The Border Trumpet*, he wrote to his editor, "These historicals always give trouble. I want to tack down as many edges as possible, though I know it is inevitable that we'll have some Indignant Reader letters."[18] One of the reasons he delayed writing about specific historical events as long as he did was that such fiction prompted arguments about accuracy that distracted readers from emotional involvement in the story. But getting the history right was more to Haycox than simply a matter of avoiding complaining and correcting letters from readers. He had a historian's curiosity and integrity: knowing the past with precision was for him a satisfaction in itself. He was particularly interested in understanding the moral temper of an era. He said, "Someone will write in and question the point that a girl would ride thirty miles unescorted with a soldier. Now this is the sort of criticism I am apt to think about because it has to do with the larger problem of morals of a certain generation" (Fargo, 178). Beneath the broad adventure action of his novels and clearly apparent in many of the short stories was a concern with right and wrong in the ordinary aspects of living. As a writer of romance he limned good and evil in broad stokes; as a writer of history he did so with modest, commonplace images.

He was a thorough researcher whether he planned to write about historical events or not. He visited locations and drew maps for reference, delved in newspaper files and musty record books in county courthouses, decorated his house with pictures of early Oregon, interviewed old-timers, and collected a library of historical information. One of his friends said, "He never accepted at second hand anything he could learn for himself" and recalled hearing him complain that the IRS questioned his expenses to travel to Arizona for background. "My gosh," said

Haycox, "do these fellows think I can write about a place before I find out every single thing there is to know about it?"[19] When doctors in Portland could not tell him much about tick fever because they saw few cases of it, Haycox wrote to a friend elsewhere in the state where cases were more common and posed a list of 14 very specific questions.[20] He wrote to the same friend to arrange a visit with an old veteran of the Seventh Cavalry who lived in the friend's neighborhood: "One of my pet preoccupations is getting Custer material, and I want to see this fellow before he dies." He wanted to ask the man when he enlisted, what an army post was like, about the routine of an ordinary day, exactly what the man wore and what equipment he used, what he thought Custer looked like, and so on.[21] He thanked a correspondent for sending him a copy of the ordinances of Jacksonville, Oregon, for he was researching that area: "It is sometimes an exasperating job. There are so many blank spots, and not really enough firsthand accounts of the way folks lived down there."[22] These examples indicate his curiosity and thoroughness.

Haycox's personal library of nearly 2,000 titles is preserved as the Ernest Haycox Memorial Library at the University of Oregon. When asked in 1938 about his reading, he replied, "I read very little outside my own technical needs. I think there are less than 200 fiction items in my library."[23] Most of that library is historical material. Many items concern the Revolutionary and Civil wars, but Haycox made only incidental use of these resources. Material dealing with the trans-Mississippi West was naturally his principal resource and the "chapter and verse" for the historical elements in his fiction. In a brief description of the library, Thomas J. Easterwood says, "Perhaps the strongest impression afforded by the titles is that here was a writer who wanted to know how people felt, thought, and acted. To that end, he collected autobiographies, rather than biographies, reminiscences and diaries, rather than formal histories, pamphlets with the juice of experience rather than sets redolent with research." Such material gave the specific information he desired:

When Haycox described a dance on the frontier, he could base his description on Thomas Hillgrove's *Complete Practical Guide to the Art of Dancing*, usually referred to as "Hallgrove's Call Book." When he took one of his characters in and out of Portland, he had a City Directory to guide his pen. When he visited the mining country, he had with him John Mullan's *Miners and Traveller's Guide*. And when he dwelt on the frontier woman—a Haycox hallmark—he had available, and obviously had read, the recollections and diaries of a shelf of western women.[24]

He was a stickler for detailed accuracy. The correspondence with Littauer regarding *The Border Trumpet*, for example, putters over the exact words of a sentry challenge and whether the Last Post or Taps was played at the burial of a soldier, and whether it was played by trumpet or bugle. Haycox meticulously sorted out such small matters, often consulting with old veterans. To help the illustrator be accurate (which was always his concern), he sent seven books from his library and some photographs. He wanted the details of dress, saddle gear, and equipment to be as authentic as possible.[25] His knowledge of such things was extraordinary. Consider this remarkable paragraph on women's fashions sent to Littauer to guide the illustrator for *Trail Smoke*:

> If I'm not mistaken 1899 is the shirtwaist era, with hair puffs and the lady's watch attached to her bosom with a fleur-de-lis pin. Her waist is still tight and the skirt, though it clings more is pretty full—and drags a little behind. We're pretty close to the Gibson girl, yet you'd find that in the western country it was a modified thing—less of hair puff and not so strong on the big hats. A good hat, if the illustrator needs one, would be a stiff-brimmed black straw, moderately wide and flat-crowned. In strict fidelity there should be hat pins. For riding, the women would be perfectly proper in a good buckskin split-skirt, or a dark cloth split-skirt. In some sections it was a daring innovation and not quite nice. A man's hat will do to go with the riding outfit. Not the ten gallon thing, which is strictly a modern rodeo accessory, but a stockman's hat, soft-brimmed, moderately wide and a creased crown that doesn't possess the exaggerated peak. But no men's pants for these particular girls. In this story and locality that sets them down a notch in the social scale. For the riding shirt, a man-style shirt cut a little better; some type of scarf optional.[26]

He does not burden his narratives with such details; it is the kind of information that, although unused, nevertheless gives his fictional re-creation of the past the stamp of authenticity. It is, to use Hemingway's analogy, the submerged portion of the iceberg.

And it was this general impression of authenticity, rather than actual facts dragged in for their own sake, that pleased readers and prompted emulation among other writers. For example, when in the late 1930s Frank Gruber decided to devote himself to westerns, there seemed to him to be 50 good mystery writers but only two readable western novelists: Ernest Haycox and Luke Short. And, as mentioned, Short has generously acknowledged his debt to Haycox. After writing some westerns, Gruber was dissatisfied. They seemed artificial. He decided he didn't know enough about the West. He read a number of Haycox's novels for the right kind of model. "Authenticity rang from every page," said Gruber. "The man was a superb writer, too." When he wrote to Haycox with his troubles, Haycox recommended factual books about the West and suggested a dealer in rare books in New York City. Gruber spent $200 on books and began to study them; a new world opened up for him. Gruber was only one writer among many who benefited from Haycox's upgrading of the western through greater authenticity.

But it wasn't simply Haycox's example of research that was important in this influence; it was the way he used the research. Any hack can crib from historical documents or employ what historian David Lavender calls "Western costuming."[27] But it takes a gifted writer to select and integrate historical facts artfully into an engaging fictional narrative. A. B. Guthrie, a master at such blending, explains that the historical novelist must not throw in undigested chunks of history. They create hurdles the reader must leap in pursuing the story. A good historical novel "has to be more than ghosts among the gimcracks. It has to be more than history faintly inhabited by figures. It has to be people, it has to be personalities, set in a time and place subordinated to them." The historical novelist must be able to read between the lines of his sources. It is not the event that is important: "it is human and individual involvement in and response to event."[28] Haycox understood these matters just as well as Guthrie, which is not to say that the challenges were always easy for him to overcome. In the process of writing *The Border Trumpet*, for example, he told Littauer in a letter, "Well, I was in a very petulant and artistic frame of mind for a couple of weeks. I read so much Arizona background that the historical angle tied me up. I had to break out of that. Now I think we've got a run-along action story with some seasoning of color and characterization."[29]

There is a danger in writing westerns of placing too much emphasis on the historical aspect: historical information can become a substitute for literary skill. Reproducing history takes the place of producing literature. Much of what goes into the cowboy of the best westerns originates in the author's imagination and not his historical notes. As Don D. Walker has pointed out, "However much it may help to tell what happened—to be historical—literature must aspire to tell what happens. Otherwise, it fails finally to be literature at all."[30] By "what happens" he means universal human meanings, what in the Aristotelian context would be called poetic truth as distinguished from historical truth. Haycox was keenly aware of the pitfalls awaiting the fiction writer who draws from history. His success in avoiding them is abundantly clear when his narratives, with their engaging characters and engrossing action, are compared with the voluminous and random historical information that went into their creation. He was an artist first and historian second.

The Discontents of Popular Success

Christine Bold detects in the fiction of Haycox's middle years an uneasiness as he tentatively diverged from his successful formulas. "During this period," she observes, "his characters become infected by their author's nervousness, and an almost modern voice appears in his fiction for the only time" (Bold, 124). The nervousness she perceives in his narratives was actually a persistent discontent voiced frequently and explicitly in his letters, particularly in those to W. F. G. Thacher, his designated artistic confidant and conscience. Thacher treasured these letters and desired after Haycox's death to use them as the core of his aborted biography. He was delighted when Little, Brown invited him to introduce a selection of them for a pamphlet titled "Dear W. F. G.," part of the promotional material for *The Earthbreakers*, published posthumously in 1952.

The letters to Thacher are a fascinating record of Haycox's inner struggles to satisfy his literary ambitions. They reveal a thoughtful intelligence that found no outlet in his fiction. When Thacher remarked in 1934 that the letters were written on a higher intellectual level than the stories, Haycox agreed and said his stories might reveal more of his thinking someday, but not until he finds a form into which he can put his deepest thoughts and feelings. It can't be done in popular fiction, he said, not in the adventure or romance genres. They allow just a few shadings and some slight inflections of the obvious. He saw only two fictional channels for what was inside him: "the cerebral type and the meaty, detailed, inclusive, panoramic novel. The cerebral sort of thing is out, for me. The other thing is what I want to do." He considered *Les Misérables* the finest example of what he aspired to. If he were to write a real novel, he said, "I want it to be a robust story, crowded, detailed, active, a good story per se. Full of brutality and tragedy; with its pieces of vivid action—and the will o' wisp of romance." But before that happens, he explained, "I've got to write the adventure-romance-popular stuff out of my system. Because of the economic necessity; and—even more important—because I've got to completely finish that mental cycle, so that I won't ever want to go back to it; so that it won't be in the back of my mind nagging me. When the shift comes—if it ever does—I shall be completely through with the thing I do now."[31] The problem, of course, was to decide exactly when he had written the popular stuff out of his system and exactly what degree of financial security would permit the shift. A further worry was whether he could finish the mental cycle without becoming habituated to its methods and conventions. And was he, after all, really capable of writing more than popular fiction? He anguished over these things for the remaining 15 years of his life, using Thacher as a sounding board.

In February 1937 he sent a copy of *Trouble Shooter* to Thacher, to whom the novel is dedicated. "It is not a bad book," he told his former teacher, "But it is not, I think, the kind of book you might think I should be writing fourteen years after school." He acknowledged that Thacher's influence has always been an insistent pressure upon him to write the best he could: "We both know what the writing job is—and the forces that limit a man, and the conscience that keeps prodding him on. It is this matter of conscience that gives me a good deal of hope. I have not yet written what I feel I could write. I'm not the sort to make excuses for what's been written, being too much a pragmatist for that. All I say is that, if good intentions and a lot of dissatisfaction are any indication at all, I may still do a good job."[32]

The letters to Thacher during these middle years express a number of quandaries, all spawned by this matter of conscience. One of those quandaries had to do with models and audience. He had avoided reading very much fiction: "My excuse has been that I've not had time. But really the reason has been that I did not wish to be influenced by others; or to unconsciously copy others." Now he was having second thoughts: perhaps in order to write quality literature he would have to study the great authors more carefully and write for their kind of audience, "for the discriminating few, the aristocrats of taste, the critically alert." But he didn't want to write for that audience; this, he said, would be affectation for him: "There's the contradiction. I can't write for them and still, if I ever really wrote a yarn that stood up, it would be exactly those people who took up the story and plugged for it." To his mind, writing for that sophisticated audience would require intellectual strategy, which was contrary to his conviction that "writing does not come from the mind. In fact a true writer is a fellow that operates in the region between his shoulders and his hips." So here was another quandary: "I am trying to build up a philosophy that will accommodate better stories than I've so far done; yet the thoughtful or philosophical attitude, for a writer, is a hell of a dangerous thing."[33]

This suspicion of "the thoughtful or philosophical attitude" was no doubt instilled in him by his career in magazine fiction, which had taught him to distrust philosophical reflection that might hinder the pace of action. But his emphasis on emotion over ideas went much deeper than that; it was basic to his view of human nature. He once confessed to Thacher: "I have an unchangeable distrust of the human mind, of reason, of intellect, or rationalism, of the power of knowledge or of man's application of knowledge." He respected facts and history and disciplined learning; "yet I cannot be convinced that man is motivated in any great degree by reason."[34] And this distrust of rationalism was fundamental to his literary credo. This is evident in two of his essays on writing from the 1940s. In the first he said, "People live by emotion and instinct rather than by reason and since the writer's business is with people, it follows that a writer is a dealer in emotion and not a purveyor of ideas. Of necessity writers must sometimes think, but it is a mistake to suppose that a writer is a first-rate intellectual, or even a second-rate thinker." In the second he argued that writers reach readers through the senses, "and since we do our work with the common feelings of people we are afraid that if we traffic too much with ideas we may become too cool and rational, and lose connection with those common feelings. It may be we are overfearful; an idea is perhaps the beefsteak from which we got our nourishment and possibly it is the writer's function to break this beefsteak down and to dissolve it by use of emotional gastric juices."[35]

What really constituted the quandary for Haycox was not the relation of ideas and emotion but his uneasiness about trying deliberately to write quality fiction. He desired to write serious fiction but felt the upgrading must evolve naturally and could not be achieved by intellectual strategy. But how was this to happen? He asked for Thacher's thoughts on "the theoretical ways a man might break through one existing mental ceiling to another. Or through one spiritual ceiling to another, for I think it is more a matter of spirit and emotion than of mind—for a writer." He thought such a break would be required before he could write about the most important matters of his inner life:

> I know what I want to do. I do not yet know how to do it. But I rather think that if I am to do it at all, it can only come by my breaking every existing pattern in my head and starting fresh. In other words I have built dykes in my head, between which the waters of imagination flow rather neatly and in orderly fashion. I think I am going to find it neces-

sary to blow up those dykes and let the water smash hell out of the peace-ful countryside. Yet perhaps I kid myself. Maybe when I blow up the dykes the overflow will be a very thin trickle. That's something I'll have to find out, and won't really rest until I do.

His quandary was deciding when to set the dynamite to those dikes. The risks involved caused prolonged hesitation. In fact, even within this let-ter he was backing away from an immediate break: "Now here I am, thinking I might have something better, but still rooted in the adven-ture yarn. Well, I'll have to stick to that because that's the type of thing I do best and like best (it is more nearly a reflection of *me* than anything else I could do; and because, also, I feel it is a mistake for me, or any writer, to forsake the discipline of some form of yarn merely to kick over the traces. The answer usually is something pretty bad." His choice at this point was to try to make the novel of adventure and romance serve his needs, although he admitted to an ego that would not allow him to be content with what he had achieved. And "being a good neighbor won't do, and the immortality a man gets by the transfer of himself to his children won't do"; he desired literary immortality. "I shall feel bitter as hell if I do not make my try. And if I make my try and fail, I shall still feel as bitter as hell. So I guess we can do nothing about it but go on. My method has always been to build up from what went before. I'm going to keep on with that method a few more years. If I can't make it work, then I'll have to try a completely fresh attack."[36]

The indecision encapsulated so dramatically in this letter appears also in his correspondence with his editors; in fact, it was exacerbated by that correspondence. His editors alternately praised his attempts to transcend formula and discouraged him from doing so. They were no more certain than he was about the line separating popular and serious fiction or about whether magazines could raise popular literary taste or were required simply to cater to it. In 1938 Littauer suggested that Haycox had reached a point where he probably ought to strike out and experi-ment now and then. Haycox responded, "I've been looking into the homely face of this exact problem for a year or two. The formula is a comfortable thing through a certain stage of a man's career. Afterwards it can be pretty deadly to him. The reverse is also true. The story that goes off the trail is swell when good but the risk is that a man gets to writing these things poorly and mistakes formlessness for Great Art." His work had relied on emotional intensity and background, but he knew that "the great thing is character, and I guess maybe that's what I have been waiting for—sufficient knowledge to make people real and human." He compared himself to the fellow "who said that after twenty years of writing for the market he was now going to let go the Facts of Life with sound and fury. My thought is: Suppose, when he lets go, there comes nothing but a small intestinal report?"[37]

Littauer replied to these reflections on the risks of moving outside formulas by saying, "All that you say about your work is interesting and sagacious. The fact is that you are in all probability a much better writer than you can afford to be. I think you have been running under wraps for many years. It would be a pity not to give yourself a gallop once in a while."[38] This was fine encouragement for Haycox's ambitions and seemed to give him the green light for experimenting. But two weeks later another member of the *Collier's* staff, Walter Davenport, wrote to him about one of the New Hope stories, the series in which he *had* taken a gallop outside the formulas: "If I were you, Erny, I would wind up these New Hope yarns and add a bit of zip to what you might write in the near future. They are perfectly swell, but I think you have almost exhausted that strain for the present."[39] Littauer himself later offered the same kind of advice. The magazine had accepted a story called "Illusion" (published as "A Girl Must Wait," 2 September 1939), but Littauer didn't like it much: "Could we, for a little while, call a truce upon these pensive laments and substitute for them some stories with movement as well as mood? . . . The fact is we have let our inventory become crowded with stories of a rather quiet appeal and we are now in immediate need of some lively exciting pieces— stories with pace and menace and strong emotional conflict rather than stories of reasoned behavior." The qualities of "Illusion" are good, he acknowledged, "but they are qualities that we must not display too often. So see if you can't give us a couple of hell-busters between now and Easter." He hopes the next serial will be good—"in the popular sense." "Everything you do is good under the aspect of eternity—a concept with which, unfortunately, we can't much concern ourselves here." Haycox replied, "Okay, okay, okay. I'll smother you in dust and sweat," and he good-naturedly added, "it is somewhat possible I have been going literary the last few stories. This is merely the inevitable itchings of spring. When I was young the tonic was a simple matter of sulphur and molasses, or boiled onions."[40] The pressure for fast-paced action came from other quarters as well. *New York Times* reviewer Jerome Parker admired Haycox's fiction but thought *Trail Town* and *Alder Gulch* moved too slowly. Haycox valued Parker's opinions, or at least respected the influence he could yield, and was thus obliged to consider his criticism.

In its 2 July 1938 issue, *Collier's* published a Haycox story about neither the past nor the West. "This Woman and This Man" is the story of a newspaper foreign correspondent traveling by train from New York to San Francisco en route to an assignment in the Philippines. He meets and falls in love with a woman along the way, the attraction is mutual, she breaks with her fiancé in San Francisco, marries the correspondent, and accompanies him abroad. Though little more than the usual magazine romance story, it was praised in separate letters from Littauer, Chenery, and Davenport. Chenery suggested that, unless he had his mind set on another period novel, he might try something more current. "I think it might be good for you because you would have to add to your technique and it might be good for us because of the variety we would be able to accept from you. . . . I don't want you to specialize too completely." In a subsequent letter he said, "We like your Westerns, both dated and undated, but I think that taking into consideration your career as well as your relationship with Collier's Weekly, it is the part of wisdom to vary your output enough to be certain that you will be able to make whatever changes time and circumstance might require."[41]

These suggestions naturally fueled Haycox's literary doubts and yearnings. "Your letter stirred up a good deal of discontent in me," he replied. "As a matter of fact I grow increasingly critical of what I do, which is perhaps a mighty fine thing for the soul but hard on the nervous system. I wish I knew what a good story was—a valid, truthful, dramatic and realistic story." He had the intent and the energy for such writing but could not see a clear way to his aims: "I'm damned if I yet know what kind of a writer I am, or ought to be, or can be."[42]

Apparently in response to Chenery's suggestions, Haycox wrote "National Beauty," a novel that remained unpublished. The main character is a young woman from Oregon who wins beauty contests on the state and national levels, gets a film contract but does not make a film, becomes disillusioned with Hollywood values and behavior, and eventually finds love with a man who has quietly watched this process of fame, disenchantment, and spiritual growth. Haycox had already written perceptively about Hollywood, and during the process of writing "National Beauty" in 1939 he spent about four months there working for Samuel Goldwyn on a preliminary script for *Seventh Cavalry,* intended to star Gary Cooper. He was fascinated by Hollywood but not taken in by any of it, as a delightfully penetrating description of his impressions written for Littauer indicates.[43] He had a remarkable gift for quickly absorbing the essential characteristics of a locale or activity.

Collier's declined "National Beauty," an outline of which remains in
the Haycox correspondence in the New York Public Library, but there is
no hint of the manuscript elsewhere. In turning it down, Littauer
explained that "it has the feeling of experimental work. I can see you
tilting the test tubes and watching reactions and shaking your head.
What you have done here is to turn your back on conventional practice,
which requires pretty definite plot effects, and attempted to sustain an
extended story by means of mood, characterization and incident. This
can be done and probably you will be able to do it some day but the
method is still too new to you." He went on to say that the story lacks
menace, lacks a villain, and needs more suspense. He discouraged
Haycox from revising it and recommended he "go back to the Western
scene."[44] Haycox did not revise it, and it was the only serial the magazine
refused from him.

This was a painful setback for Haycox, but he took it with good
grace. He replied that he had not "crawled into a deep cave to brood
over the bitter fate of authors in a mass-production world" but had had
to "stand erect in the chill wind." He wrote, "Since this is one of my children, I'm naturally reluctant to admit it is non compos mentis. All I'll
concede is that it's just a little shy before company. However, in a terrif-
ic bust of frankness, I'll admit your judgment was sound in rejecting it.
That last sentence came out inch at a time, under pressure." He
explained that the novel was an experiment in which he had deliberately
turned away from the strongly plotted action of his westerns, but he had
failed to find an adequate substitute: "My trouble is that my modern
people do not answer to primitive instincts. They're parlor people, afraid
to express human emotion. In order to get them alive I seem to find it
necessary to lay them back in history somewhere. Then all bets are off
and anything can happen. This shows up in my plotting. I'm unable to
bring them to the point of all-hell-busts-loose—the moderns, I mean. I
can't find physical action and intrigue that is logical to me." Because he
could not face a major revision of "National Beauty," he chose as his
recourse "going back to the old south forty and do a western." He concluded the letter by explaining that the real problem was that he had so
far found "no pattern in modern life, either fictional or real." All he saw
was people bustling about in a mindless and mistaken search for
"Happiness": "It's an age of Montgomery Ward gadgets, mental and
physical, and a good rain would reduce all their glossy surfaces and fancy
stitching to a mess of gray pulp." He had mentioned in an earlier letter
to Littauer his feeling that something was missing in modern life:

"Without wishing to be mystical I think it must be faith and positive belief. Any kind of faith, any kind of positive belief, even if nothing better than faith in man's regeneration through a buttermilk diet."[45] Although he continued to write short stories about modern life, this aborted serial was his last attempt at a novel set in the present. His imagination and moral vision were better attuned to the frontier West. There he found, or at least he thought he found, evidence of the faith and integrity he felt were lacking in modern life.

In mentioning "the lately lamented serial" "National Beauty" to Chenery, Haycox said, "I tried to write a story without conventional plot. By contrast the next one will probably show plot scaffolding at every corner. This is indeed a very mystifying profession, or trade."[46] This last sentence may refer to the difficulties of writing good stories, but it also expresses his puzzlement with the contradictory messages from his editors: experiment, but provide for our formula needs; develop your gifts for serious fiction, but give us a couple of hell-busters between now and Easter. Haycox could not help but wonder whether he was part of a literary profession or a publishing trade.

The same desires and doubts expressed in the letters to Thacher and *Collier's* appear also in Haycox's correspondence with C. Raymond Everitt, his editor at Little, Brown, the company that routinely bought his serials to publish in book form. When Everitt praised *Trail Town*, Haycox replied that he had really wanted to make the book as much a portrait of a trail town as an action story would permit, and he would like someday to do the trail town idea again in all its social and economic shades. "I look with a good deal of yearning at the solid historical," he said, describing a big novel that would cover the whole era from the Civil War to Teddy Roosevelt. Everitt was enthusiastic about the idea, noting that the interest in historical novels remained undiminished even though many were being written. He said that Little, Brown would extend itself financially for such a project, though "naturally this would not be anywhere near enough to take care of missing a serial sale." But, he suggested, the successful publication of such a book might bring returns outside of royalties that could more than compensate for the loss of the serial sale of a regular western.

Despite such enticements, Haycox was not yet ready to make the gamble. He thought it nearly impossible to straddle simultaneously the novel and serial forms. The project would take a year of research and interfere with his regular schedule. He had discussed the possibility from time to time with his agent, who naturally discouraged him from breaking the very successful serial routine. That, he said, was half the problem. The other half was that even though there is no substantial book market for a straight western (this was before the paperback boom), he did not propose to take an "artistic point of view" and write something long, heavy, and uninteresting. He explained that "my conception of a story is one which contains strong characterization, plus background, plus strong action throughout. I cannot write deliberate Social Significance, and do not want to. There must be dust and grunting in my stories, out of which the Social Significance finds its own sweet way, if any."[47]

These were legitimate considerations for a magazine writer at the apex of his success, but knowing the nature of his artistic ambitions and discontents, we might detect a note of fear and rationalization. This was 1941. He was to wrestle with these matters for a few more years before forsaking the lucrative serial market.

Chapter Five
The Final Years

The Short Stories

By 1943 Haycox had achieved his principal aspirations in the magazine market. During this year his serialized novels appeared in both *Collier's* and the *Saturday Evening Post*, the two leading outlets for such fiction. Breaking into the pages of the *Post* had been his aim for 20 years, and he was pleased to do so with *Bugles in the Afternoon*, perhaps his best historical western. This year also marked the beginning of a new and final phase of his career. In the last seven years of his life the quantity of his work diminished while he agonized over improving its quality by diverging from the very methods and conventions he had worked so long and hard to perfect. After 1943 he published only one serial and one novel before his death; one serial and two novels appeared posthumously. In the preceding seven years he had written 12 serials including the unpublished "National Beauty." And the number of published stories similarly declined from 49 during 1937–43 to 25 during 1944–50.

There were a number of reasons for this reduced productivity. During the war he was offered a commission in his World War I infantry unit. His family dissuaded him from accepting, and he instead became the chairman of his local draft board. This was just one of many civic activities to distract him from writing during the 1940s. His wife described him as being about four men rolled into one. As a popular speaker and toastmaster, he was a member of the American Legion and the Portland Chamber of Commerce, elected to its board of directors in 1947. He was also on the boards of the Oregon State Library, the Oregon Historical Society, and the local area council of the Boy Scouts of America. He served as president of the Portland Rotary Club and as director of the Portland Rose Festival Association. He founded the Oregon Freelance Club, a professional writers group. Active in the Republican party, he was sought after for the state chairmanship; and there was also talk for a while of a gubernatorial candidacy. He declined these political opportunities for the sake of his writing, but he did so with some regret because he thought he would have enjoyed them. He served two terms as president of the University of Oregon Alumni Association and led the fund-raising for building the Erb Memorial Building. He also took a turn as president of the University Dads' Club. Because of his keen interest in Oregon history, he helped the highway department compose and locate historical markers. In 1947 he went to Greece as a representative for the United States Mission for Aid to Greece. Without leaving Portland, he did two treatments for Hollywood films and became involved with film-maker Walter Wanger in plans for a multifilm venture—plans that never materialized but required time and attention.

In addition to these civic and business activities, he signed a contract with Little, Brown to do an anthology of western writing. With his usual enthusiasm, he began an exhaustive plan of reading. He wanted to include both fiction and nonfiction and provide a cross section of western history, morals, economics, and society. The task as he conceived it was too time consuming, and after two years he requested and received a release from the contract. His interest in the West was also manifested in 10 reviews of books on western history done for the *New York Times* from 1944 to 1946.

These activities were enough to diminish the productivity of even an unusually energetic and disciplined professional like Haycox, but they were not the principal reason he published less during those last seven years. The main reason was the challenging and often frustrating process of giving up the serial market and devoting himself to novels about Oregon history.

Haycox's late short stories provide an index to a number of transitions that were taking place in his art: shifts in subject matter, aims, and techniques. Cowboys and romantic cattle-kingdom formulas disappear and are replaced by pioneers and more realistic—even naturalistic—depiction of the westering experience. Settings in a generalized West give way to specific locations in Oregon. The spotlight shifts from male to female characters, and the frontier woman's perspective receives increased attention. Gender conflict becomes a recurrent theme, and sexuality, though kept within the confines of the family-magazine tastes of the time, receives increased and more explicit treatment. But at the same time that the heat is turned up under sexual passion, kindness and consideration are presented as the most important elements in marriage; physical passion is not enough. The early fiction often ended in marriage; these late stories explore the conditions of marriage—primarily marriage under the stress of frontier living. The endings are not always neat and happy, and without stretching for what he scorned as "Significance," Haycox achieves richer thematic implications and psychological complexity. Moreover, the individualism glorified in the earlier narratives is modulated by a recognition of community obligation: pioneering is presented as a cooperative endeavor.

"Custom of the Country" (*Collier's*, 29 May 1948) is a good example of such changes. Rose Ann Talbot, a 20-year-old woman living in Portland when it consisted of only a dozen houses, is disturbed to see Hobert Walling, a disagreeable farmer of 30, making arrangements to marry Sarah Lord, a girl of 14. It is obvious that Hobart simply wants a household drudge and the extra half-section of land being married will allow him. He has already used an Indian woman and sent her back to her village when he was dissatisfied. Sarah's parents are poor and uneducated and view the marriage as a way of being rid of a mouth to feed and gaining a prosperous son-in-law. Sarah's consent is the kind to be bought with a bag of candy; she comes from the backwoods of Missouri and knows little of life except that girls are to be wives and mothers as soon as physically able. Rose Ann complains to her father about this situation and suggests they take Sarah in so she can experience the joys of youth and love rather than being turned into a household slave whose vitality will be sapped before she is 25. Her father says that it is the usual arrangement on the frontier, that Sarah couldn't expect anything better, and that they have no business interfering. Rose Ann, however, is determined to prevent the marriage. She visits Hawley McBride, a young saw mill operator, complains of the marriage plan, and hints that if Mr. Lord had a job he would not have to bargain his daughter away. McBride suggests that it's the Lord family's affair and not theirs. "He was like her father," Rose Ann thinks; "he could not see what she saw." Nevertheless, she learns next day that McBride has hired Lord. Unfortunately, this does not alter the marriage plan, but Rose Ann realizes that she has made McBride understand, at least a little bit.

She then consults with another woman in the community, Mrs. Ellenwood, who tells her, "You know, Rose Ann, that men run the world. You're a girl and you've no power to change men's minds." Rose Ann replies, "but a man might help me." Mrs. Ellenwood, sensing the young woman's determination, says, "Well, Rose Ann, maybe we're so close to the earth we don't see the sky. Life's very hard in a new country and people get coarse sometimes. If it's in your heart to help Sarah, then you've got to do it." With that bit of encouragement, Rose Ann enters the male domain of the store, where Walling is talking with other men.

She knows the conversation is not meant for her ears, but she walks boldly to the counter. Sensing Walling's eyes on her, she asks him what he is staring at. He is offended: "Go home where you belong and don't break into men's talk." "You," she replies, "are a fat lunk of a creature. Do you ever shave or ever wash? You smell like a barn. And here you are, telling me what I ought to do. I shall stay here. You do the going." He responds angrily, "By God, get back to your place before I take you for another kind of woman." She slaps him, and when he raises a hand, slaps him again, and then reaches for an ax handle. The storekeeper steps in to restrain Walling, who then threatens to go to her father. She says she will shoot him if he steps into their cabin. As she leaves, she knows she has offended the other men: "All men stuck together—they said nothing but they created an air of disapproval."

Her father questions her about the incident at supper, and McBride comes by with the same inquiry. Later McBride thrashes Walling and tells him to forget about Sarah Lord. When Walling in bewilderment asks what started all this, McBride says, "You just ran into some opposition," and smiles to himself at the thought of Rose Ann. He later confronts Rose Ann with her scheming and asks why she picked him for her fighting. "'Because,' she said, pleasantly matter-of-fact with her answer, 'you're the only one who can whip him.'"

This delightfully skillful story displays how far Haycox had come from the male-centered cowboy story in which women play an insignificant role. Although to be accurate, Haycox himself, in contrast to the average writer of westerns, began enlarging the characterization of women quite early in his career. The nature of his evolution in the treatment of the female perspective is indicated by comparing the way the phrase "custom of the country" is used in this story with how it is used in his first novel. In *Free Grass* the phrase appears several times to describe the male code of the West that is the value center of the book, particularly the custom of scrupulously minding one's own business. In "Custom of the Country," however, it is that very masculine code that is brought under critique by a female perspective.

According to W. H. Hutchinson, "Woman in the 'western' was a sawdust doll, and the tags used to depict her character were obvious"; the pure maiden and the fallen woman, for example. This simplification allowed the reader to focus on the action "without getting petticoats in his mind and thus complicating the author's task."[1] In general, women in westerns are there to be rescued and protected. They sometimes serve to say revealing things about the hero that male characters could not say.

Primarily they serve as a reward for the hero, a certification of the heroic action that is the central interest of the narrative. Haycox abandoned such stereotypes before the end of the 1920s. The fact is that he was preoccupied for years with male and female strengths in relation to the West. He believed in a profound connection between frontier and gender issues. The phrase "it's a man's world" has often been used to refer to the frontier West; Haycox himself used it a number of times. But he went on to consider these questions: If it was a man's world, exactly where did the woman fit in? What were her restrictions and opportunities, her burdens and joys? How did she view the westering adventure? He read enough firsthand accounts—many by women—to know that pioneer women were often as determined and resilient as the men. They worked with men in the labors of settlement with a quiet degree of equality. Their strength and confidence were often so great that they treated their men with a motherly tolerance. Frequently their frontier femininity in part shaped frontier masculinity: some men exaggerated their own masculinity in order to neutralize women's power over them. On the pioneer trail men suffered hardships and pain unknown to them back East in their jobs as teachers, clerks, and small-town farmers. This both hardened and weakened them. As wives revealed in diaries, the trials often seemed more traumatic for the men than for the women. And as though to protect themselves, men adopted a new image of manhood. But neither the belief in the inferiority of woman nor the worship of her presumed angelic nature developed naturally out of the pioneer experience. Both were imported from the East with other Victorian furnishings, mainly after the Civil War.

Women in Haycox's late fiction say such things as these to men: "You don't know women well enough to take them as they are," or "Ah, you're reading things into me you want to read, making a mystery of nothing. Men do that more than women. That's why they get disappointed sooner than women. A husband expects too much. Then he finds it's not there, and he quits expecting anything." This is part of the recurring theme of gender conflict in Haycox's stories: men either expect too much of women or too little. Near the end of *Bugles in the Afternoon* the predatory womanizer Edward Garnett, before dying on the battlefield, confesses his true understanding of women: "The earth is a woman and, like all women, stronger than any man can be. Men are the vessels God made to carry illusions. Women are the realists; they are the strength of the race. They love, they hate, they bear. They pray and they sin. But they are stronger than love or sin." These sentiments echo in his

letters and late narratives. In fact, "The Earth Is a Woman" was the preliminary title of *The Earthbreakers*.

In explaining the motive behind "Cry Deep, Cry Still," one of his pioneer women stories, Haycox notes that history has been written mostly
by men and that the woman's perspective is missing. Men, he says, are
mainly interested in politics, action, and large events and are consequently poor observers of small daily matters. Many women are superior
"in the business of seeing the small details which, after all, constitute the
true picture of daily life." To illustrate his point, he quotes two diary
entries made the same day by members of the same wagon train. The
man wrote, "Made 14 miles today, camped by the river in the rain, shot
a deer, very tired." The woman wrote, "We pitched camp in the driving
rain. The fire wouldn't burn and the smoke was so strong in my eyes
that I cried. I couldn't make the beans boil and all the time I heard Mrs.
Jackson's dying baby crying in the next wagon. Out on the river the
waves were four feet high and I didn't know how we could ever survive
going down that terrible place." (This entry is subtly integrated into the
first chapter of *The Earthbreakers*.) Haycox adds his opinion that women
bore most of the work of pioneering, and it broke many of them, but
those who survived were spiritually very strong: "That's why I wrote
'Cry Deep, Cry Still.'"[2]

There is a statue near the University of Oregon Library called *The
Pioneer Mother,* with which Haycox was familiar. It depicts a woman seat-
ed reflectively in a chair, a book in her hand, her thumb holding her
place. The 1932 inscription by the sculptor, Burt Brown Barker, reads,
"Others have perpetuated her struggles; I want to perpetuate the peace
that followed her struggles. Others have perpetuated her adventure; I
want to perpetuate the spirit which made the adventure possible, and
the joy which crowned her declining years as she looked upon the fruits
of her labor and caught but a faint glimpse of what it will mean to pos-
terity." It is reasonable to assume Haycox's affinity for this statue, but,
unlike the sculptor, he was one who perpetuated the pioneer woman's
struggles and adventure. His stories of the settlement of Oregon, particularly the cluster concerning the Mercy family,[3] constitute his tribute to
the pioneer mother.

Haycox likened the writing of these stories to "drilling test holes
into the field to locate a seepage of oil."[4] He was prospecting for the
subjects and methods to use in his projected novels about Oregon history. But the stories succeed in their own right, and, particularly in
their depth of female characterization, they succeed better than the

serialized novels. When his editor at Little, Brown pointed this out to him, Haycox agreed: "Hitherto I have always written a better short story than a novel—in point of characterization." He explained three reasons for this. First, he was always aware of space limitations in composing a short story: "It is a precision job requiring short, intense strokes. I work hard to achieve much in minimum space." Second, the serialized novel, he said, "has always been to me a run along thing with emphasis on action and suspense. The plot frequently overpowered the people; for speed and feeling were frequently more important to me than people. But by virtue of its shortness . . . the short story must center on people or it is a failure." And third, the compression forced him to use suggestion and implication in portraying both major and minor characters: "The implications opened doors. I couldn't go through the doors and explore further in terms of scenes, but frequently the reader's imagination went through the doors." He further explained that "in my serials it frequently happened that my leading people were standard dimension pieces straight out of the lumber yard, as is so frequently the case in an action story. I did not feel a necessity of digging into them layer after layer; to have done so would have slowed the action beyond serial limits."[5]

Haycox received little encouragement to write about frontier women. He had made his mark as a writer of cowboy stories, and those marketing his fiction were more interested in sales than in his literary development. During 1949 when the paperback industry was in its infancy, a program of publishing collections of his stories began. The plan evolved into three volumes dealing, respectively, with law enforcement, struggle for the land (army and Indians, cattlemen and homesteaders), and the struggle of men and women on the frontier (*Rough Justice, By Rope and Lead*, and *Pioneer Loves*). The director of Pocket Books was very skeptical about the third volume and agreed to it only if the first two succeeded. And when that volume appeared (consisting mostly of stories about pioneer women), the cover illustration and blurbs conveyed the impression that it was filled with cowboy action. In the years since Haycox's death, his heirs have encountered the same reluctance on the part of paperback publishers to reprint those of his stories that stray from cowboy formulas. And when such stories have been reprinted, they have been marketed as category westerns. For example, the collection *Prairie Guns*, with a cowboy cover illustration and subtitled "Stories of Pursuit and Danger on the Plains of the Pioneer West," is actually devoid of pursuit and danger of the cowboy-formula kind.

The focus on women was only one of the ways he strayed from cowboy formulas in the late stories. Another was his shift from the self-contained cowboy loner to mutually dependent pioneers. Inevitably our memory of western history becomes oversimplified and shaped by popular media. Currently the distortion—especially in western films—seems to emphasize mindless violence in a savage, amoral society. But anyone who examines the pioneering period will find that there were a good many selfless, gentle characters who belie the violent-entrepreneurial caricatures. Writers who neglect this fact and emphasize killers and exploiters underestimate the breadth of the western experience and leave us poorer.[6] Rather than underestimating the breadth of that experience, Haycox had a keen and abiding interest in it. That interest fueled his literary ambitions during the 1940s.

Another group of stories from this period deserves at least brief mention. They are modern romances, most of them set in a small town near Portland. The war created a shortage of magazine manuscripts as writers volunteered or were drafted. Light romances with a hometown, patriotic flavor were in demand as relief from grim war news. Haycox, always alert to market needs, and welcoming an opportunity for variety in his writing, supplied the demand. Some of these stories are largely romantic fluff, but they display Haycox's populist values and his preoccupation with the continuity of the frontier ethos. And they reveal a movement toward more intense and comprehensive treatment of sexual passion.

As a writer of short stories, Haycox found the magazine market generally congenial to his interests and tastes. He chafed under the conventions of serialized novels and waffled for years over the decision to give them up and pursue his artistic ambitions with straight novels; with short stories, however, he found opportunities and latitude he could live with. He liked writing straightforward stories for a general audience. As he told Thacher, "I cannot take bizarre and tortured people and make stories out of them by means of shock appeal or clinical analysis." Neither could he be a propagandist for the oppressed or for a shining future world: "I will take that bus only to the first transfer point; then I get off, for I know damned well that bus never will reach its glittering destination."[7] He recorded at some length his attitudes about writing stories for the *Post* in a 1948 letter to a correspondent who inquired about just that matter. He explained that the *Post* had a large audience and was obliged to select stories that treat fundamental values. More specialized literary magazines could go in for "the so-called 'significant' tale" and "delve into the aberrations of this race," but such specialization and accent on "odd literary preoccupations" could mean an even more slanted policy than was found in general-circulation magazines. The *Post,* he said, catered to a general audience, and "the average man likes steak, mashed potatoes and gravy, apple pie and coffee. But the odd thing about this fellow is that his tastes are catholic. He also likes olives, French wines, crepes suzette, eggs à la mandarin and chow mein. You'd find, I think, on inspection of *Post*'s pages, the definite attempt to supply many kinds of stories for many kinds of appetites." As for the matter of taboos, he observed that what would offend average people in reference to religion, politics, and morals would offend the *Post*. He quoted what one editor was supposed to have said concerning the morals of a certain heroine: "She cannot commit that act on our pages—but of course we can't be responsible for her actions between installments." Still, Haycox admitted to feeling himself unpinched by such standards: "If I accept the *Post* taboos, it is not because I accept them for *Post*'s sake, but rather that I accept them for my own sake." He said he was not troubled that the magazine was conservative in the sense of conserving tested values and feeling responsibility in its use of words.

He further claimed that in writing for such magazines as *Post* he was not undertaking a story from the point of view of a deliberate formula. He was convinced that a good story would find a market and would not necessarily need a simple happy ending. Because Haycox is usually classified as a formula writer, his views on formula writing are worth considering:

> Every writer has a certain field in which he does his best work, and it usually happens that he restricts himself to this field. He has certain themes he likes best, and repeats them. There are certain kinds of people he understands better than others, and these will recur in his stories. He has certain preferred methods of telling a story, and he often leans on certain tricks, consciously or unconsciously. Beyond this we must add one last and important qualification: A writer has limitations and though he may dream of the perfect story, he can only do what he can do. . . . It's my impression that emphasis on formula has ruined more stories than it's made. There is a pattern to a good story, but no pattern is worth much without the final ingredient, which is the writer's own enthusiasm for his project. If he believes it and feels it as he writes it, he's on the right track. Without such belief the story will be a pedestrian performance, no matter how perfect the technique or how sure-fire the formula.[8]

Some of Haycox's late stories represent the best of that era's popular magazine fiction. They resulted from a fortunate blending: an expert writer with enthusiasm for his subject, respect for his market, and concern with artistic pattern over mere formula.

The Serials

The Wild Bunch, appearing during the fall of 1943, was the last Haycox serial to appear in *Collier's*. It was also his final cowboy novel and reveals both how much his patterns for such narratives remained the same over the years and how much they changed. It has many elements typical of the western in general and characteristic of Haycox's westerns in particular. The hero is strong, taciturn, slightly melancholy, and adheres to the code Haycox portrayed repeatedly as the wellspring of the western ethos. In making a journey to avenge the death of his sister, he becomes involved in the usual range war. According to Haycox pattern, he is attracted to two women and must eventually choose between them. The reader familiar with Haycox's fiction will recognize his distinctive versions of the fistfight, the poker metaphors, the outlaw sanctuary, the prolonged pursuit in mountain country, the East-West contrast, and the showdown. Other Haycox hallmarks include plenty of action at night, the hero's philosophical reflections on the starry sky, a large cast of characters, and pride as the principal motivating force for both good and evil. And this listing of typical characteristics could easily be extended.

The interesting thing about *The Wild Bunch,* however, is not its typicality but rather the imaginative developments within the typical. Commercial requirements compelled Haycox to repeat patterns, but he found room within them for a degree of artistic innovation. In a letter to Raymond Everitt of Little, Brown, he expressed his attitudes about working within western formulas and at the same time improving them. Everitt had commissioned Tom Lea to do a poster of Haycox Country to be used in bookstores and on the jackets of Haycox books. Lea was a first-rate artist who would later distinguish himself further as a novelist of the Southwest (*The Brave Bulls, The Wonderful Country*). Haycox was pleased with the poster and thought it hit exactly the right note: "action and out-of-doors, but a cut or two above the lurid and melodramatic which has so tarred and feathered the western." He went on to explain that "bringing the western out of the kitchen into the parlor is a damned difficult feat, for if you too obviously trim the story for the parlor crowd the old standby reader in the kitchen isn't going to like it. The kitchen crowd has been our small and faithful support. We can't afford to lose it. But if we are to get volume we've got to break over to other reader classifications—and there's the quandary." He said that for his part he worked hard at ways to improve characterization and invent fresher scenes: "For a fellow in the adventure field the big thing, outside of characterization, is inventiveness; to create sharp, clear scenes, to bust the villain on the chin in new ways. Or ways that seem to be new."[9] In attempting to increase the quality of his westerns, his strategy—as these statements suggest—was not to abandon the formulas or invent radically new plots but to enrich characterization and be inventive within the proven patterns. *The Wild Bunch* is a good example of this strategy.

The standard conflicts and players are present in this novel, and the plot involves the usual romance and adventure; but the reader's interest is really on psychological motivations and interactions. What is happening inside the characters is more important than the action itself. Haycox, in other words, uses formula as a means rather than an end. The physical action is engrossing, but the substance of the narrative is its examination of violence, pride, moral complexity, need for community, and gender conflict.

How far Haycox has come in enhancing formula elements is indicated in the following examples. The two-women motif is standard, but the women in this case are far from stereotypes. Both are strong, independent, and in positions of authority with men at their command. One of them is a particularly complex blending of good and bad qualities. The issue of power in the sexual relationship with the hero is more significant than in the earlier fiction, and the erotic element in the physical description of the women is stronger. The novel ends conventionally with a showdown, but in this case the hero deliberately wounds rather than kills the villain, even though the man had murdered his best friend. And, in a particularly atypical twist, the villain ends up with one of the heroines.

The most interesting modification of a formula element is the way Haycox transforms the chase into a symbolic journey of redemptive self-discovery. With considerable literary skill and subtlety, he uses characters and events symbolically. And the novel, unlike the average cowboy story, will bear careful literary analysis. Here are some highlights that could be addressed in such analysis. Frank Goodnight at the midpoint of the novel shoots the man who has seduced and abandoned his sister. At the point of death, that man complains, "A man ought to be free. But he can't do without a woman and the woman takes his freedom. Your sister smiled back at me, Goodnight. Now I'm dyin' because of it. Is that fair?" Frank is disturbed by what he has done, and the remainder of the novel, consisting largely of an extended chase in the mountains, becomes a transforming journey of redemption. As he is pursued by the wild bunch, Frank experiences illuminating encounters. These encounters do not further the action plot; their function is entirely symbolic.

The process begins immediately after he has achieved his revenge, when he observes a drunk lying in the dust of the street. He reflects that there must have been good in the man—dreams and possibilities as well as evil. "He came from the same place as the stars. Then he fell and a star went out. Why is that?" Another dimension is added when deep in the forest he finds a decaying cabin. "Near it was a square patch of ground enclosed by stakes; and centered in the patch was the mark of a grave, its headboard, once white, lying rotten upon the earth. A pine stood hard by and when he raised his eyes he saw an ax imbedded in the bark. Once, long ago, some man had driven it full into the wood and had walked away, and had never returned." This striking scene is unrelated to the chase, but it hints at the hero's growing understanding of human love, dreams, effort, misfortune, and transience.

After resisting an opportunity to destroy his pursuers when they are vulnerably exposed on a narrow cliff trail, Frank encounters a young fugitive who offers to help him; but Frank refuses to draw the young man into his troubles. He senses that the boy is teetering on the edge of outlawry and tells him, "A man was meant to be free. If he isn't free he isn't anything. You have taken away your own freedom. You have put yourself in your own jail and the sentence is entirely up to you." He would like to tell him that "an outlaw is a man alone—and no man alone is free," but he knows that one doesn't learn that by being told; it must be learned by experience: "By sitting alone at a campfire night upon night and watching the stars and seeing beauty there, and feeling wonders in the wind, and tasting the greatness of the earth—and having no living soul to share these discoveries with." Of course the boy's situation parallels Frank's own, and the lesson it holds is one that he, too, is learning. As he rides on, thoughts of the young man come back to worry him and are blended with thoughts of his family, friends, the man he killed, and the woman who has excited his interest.

Soon after this Frank encounters one of his pursuers prostrate with a heart attack and abandoned by his fellow outlaws. The man is now too sick to feel hatred: "He had reached for his gun and then, as a gesture of something no longer important, he had dropped his arm. It was a strange thing, this change, this helplessness, this lack of interest. It was as though the man had been jerked by strings, his actions not of his own will; and then the strings broke and he had collapsed and was nothing." Frank gives him what little aid he can and promises to send someone for him. "Who'd come?" the man asks. "Who'd give a damn?" The man fears being alone and observes, "Funny thing. You're the same as any other man. Why was I in the pack that chased you?" He says the situation they are part of is no good: "Look at me and see what it comes to. We're livin' like dogs and this is a dog's end. Take a look at me. It'll happen to you. Better get out." The young fugitive represents the beginning of the outlaw trail, and this man signifies its end. These scenes are stages in a mythic forest journey of self-discovery that culminates in the hero's return to the open plain, to the human community, and to a showdown in which he refuses to kill the man who murdered his best friend and threatens his own life. This is cowboy fiction both conventional and unconventional at the same time. It was about as far as Haycox could go in exercising literary artistry within a rigidly conventionalized genre.

Bugles in the Afternoon was a significant step in Haycox's movement from category westerns toward historical fiction about the West. It was highly successful in the *Post* and sold well in hardcover. It continues as one of his best-known and most admired novels. Even Bernard DeVoto pronounced it sound history and "almost a good novel."[10] DeVoto's "almost" is an expression of his bias toward realism and his distaste for romance. Measured by standards of realism or "serious" literature, the novel will inevitably be judged a near miss, for it was, after all, written for serialization in a popular magazine. Moreover, Haycox was self-consciously writing romance and preferred it over realism. The terms *realism* and *romance* are of course slippery and problematic; they obviously meant very different things to DeVoto and Haycox. What romance meant to Haycox is indicated in this statement to Thacher concerning what he was aiming for in one of his later novels: "Condensed down it is much beauty, much pain, much cruelty and aimlessness and self-inflicted defeat, an indifferent world, a brotherhood which men feel yet scarcely are aware of, irony and disillusion, yet in spite of that a hunger that never dies out." He went on to admit that "I am of course a romantic and can be nothing else; and for many years the knowledge of that stopped me, since I have felt that buoyancy and hope are not the qualities by which strong stories are written. In that I have been mistaken. Most of us possess the romantic streak. It is this which makes us struggle, and makes us so keenly feel the tragedy of defeat. This seems to be the essential story of life—starting so full of hope and ending either in misery or indifference or incompleteness, and knowing it, and still knowing it might have been better, or wishing it might have been better."[11] Obviously romance for him did not connote naïveté and sentimentality. On the contrary, his romantic perspective sees life whole but confronts it with faith: "faith in the unknown, in ourselves, in some

moral code or in some system of ethics, in a way of living, in a destiny—
faith in something."[12] Measured by standards of romanticism of this sort,
Bugles in the Afternoon is a successful novel.

Kern Shafter, the protagonist, has lost such faith. He comes to Fort
Lincoln in the Dakota Territory in 1875 and enlists as a private after
being out of the army for 10 years. He had been an officer in the Civil
War. A woman's betrayal and a fight with an unscrupulous officer who
caused the betrayal, Edward Garnett, had caused his bitterness and his
separation from the military. Unfortunately, Garnett happens to be at
Fort Lincoln, and the conflict between the two men resumes. This time
they are rivals for the affection of Josephine Russell, the daughter of a
shopkeeper. The story of this triangle, together with several subplots, is
blended with the historical account of the Battle of the Little Bighorn.
Because Shafter has been hurt by a woman and tries to put his life
together in a world of men, gender conflict is a central theme explicitly
discussed by the main characters. And, as might be expected, this narrative written during World War II portrays courage, duty, and comradeship in a positive light. The hero is not with Custer at the end but is a
survivor of one of the accompanying battles. Rather than killing the villain in a showdown, he aids him when he is fatally wounded in battle.
Kern Shafter learns stern lessons about the emptiness of glory, the ambi-
guities of moral behavior, and the illusoriness of human dreams; but he
regains that anchoring faith in life that was the heart of Haycox's
romanticism.

The novel includes more historical background and perhaps more
philosophical reflection than the serials in *Collier's*. In marketing it,
Little, Brown took pains to present it as historical fiction and gave it a
major advertising push. The first sketches for the cover were rejected
because they had too much flavor of the western, and the editor instruct-
ed that the phrase "an historical novel" appear on the front cover and
spine. Both the *Post* and Little, Brown were concerned that the historical
material was accurate. Haycox was able to satisfy their questions, and
one of the current Custer experts, Fred Dustin, read the manuscript and
pronounced it accurate. Additional praise came from other authors of
books on Custer. The truth is that Haycox himself was a knowledgeable
Custer interpreter. No books in his library were more heavily annotated
than those dealing with Custer and the events of the summer of 1876.
Haycox was keenly interested in the subject for many years and accumulated a great deal of source material. According to historian Richard
Etulain, "The result of his research was an historical novel based on solid

documentation in primary and secondary sources and a work that advanced a notable interpretation of a complex man and his involvement in a series of controversial events" (Etulain 1954, 141).

A number of Haycox's distinctive strengths come together in *Bugles in the Afternoon*. Kern Shafter is the kind of western-code hero Haycox had perfected over the years: physically strong but refined in sentiment; admirable in character but with interesting inner conflicts; firm in his integrity but capable of change. He is well suited to convey the author's distinctive vision of western character, a vision that strongly appealed to wartime America and continues to satisfy many despite current political-cultural attacks on the western genre. Another strength is the novel's vivid representation—of landscape, atmospheric conditions, clothing, customs, activities, and material objects. The brilliant description of the stage coach trip in the first chapter epitomizes the novel's detailed evocative power: we see, feel, taste, and smell that travel. This air of specific authenticity is a characteristic achievement of Haycox fiction. Other strengths include a general plausibility of character and action; an engaging blending of internal and external conflicts; an intensity in male-female relationships, often achieved by brief dialogue rich in implication; fluent action narrative; and a large cast of individualized characters.

Canyon Passage, serialized in the *Post* during the first months of 1945, was the last Haycox novel to appear in magazine installments. Its setting is the discovery of gold on the Rogue River in 1849 and the ensuing war with the Rogue Indians. Unlike *Bugles in the Afternoon*, this narrative does not attempt a complete and accurate portrayal of the conflict with Indians. That conflict simply serves, along with gold mining, as background for romantic action shaped by the theme that new land means new opportunities. In treating Oregon history, Haycox was returning to a subject that had interested him since his first treatments of it in his early stories. He was not a regional writer in a strict sense. In fact, he suspected that a self-conscious search for regionalism diminished rather than enlarged the stature of a community.[13] But Oregon obviously was at the core of his interests and affections.

And *Canyon Passage* provided an opportunity for the people of Oregon to honor Haycox and his fiction. When a Universal Pictures film adaptation was produced by Walter Wanger in 1946, the governor of Oregon, Earl Snell, flew to Hollywood and officially requested that the film be premiered in Portland. That premiere attracted many Hollywood celebrities, and the festivities included parades, a testimonial dinner for Haycox (featuring Oregon foods), and the presentation of an honorary degree from Lewis and Clark College, with the governor and movie people in attendance. A special showing of the film was arranged in Washington, D.C., for the Oregon Congressional delegation and their families. Wayne Morse, colorful Oregon senator, praised the film on the Senate floor; the speech went into the Congressional Record and was printed in newspapers across the country.[14] All of this must have gratified Haycox, who had been unselfish in his service to the Portland community. He admitted to Thacher, "The desire to get out and shine before my fellow man has always been rather strong; and there is some do-good in me."[15]

Haycox's editors at Little, Brown likewise gave the novel special consideration. The first sketches for the jacket were rejected because they suggested cattle country rather than Oregon forest. The artist was told, "We wish to avoid having this book classed as a western story, which it will be unless we get some design that definitely raises it out of this class." Yet in a second letter he was told that Haycox was the foremost writer in this class.[16] Little, Brown wanted a jacket design commensurate with their estimate of the quality of the writing. But in reality, the editors at Little, Brown were as uncertain as those at *Collier's* about how to classify Haycox fiction or rate its quality. Conventional literary evaluation has never been certain what to make of very good writers in genres considered subliterary. Writers like Haycox, Hammett, and Chandler confound the conventional standards of literary judgment.

Canyon Passage can be seen as a transitional stage between the cowboy and the pioneer story. The protagonist, Logan Stuart, is the typical Haycox code hero in most respects, but he lacks the melancholy and fatalism of the cowboy heroes. He minds his own business and is nobly taciturn to an extent, but he also is willing to mix in the affairs of others and has a more positive and ambitious temperament. Unlike the cowboy heroes, he doesn't view himself as caught in the old familiar cycles and rituals of violence. He is a kind a pioneer rather than a gunslinger, an entrepreneur rather than a drifter. When Haycox turned to stories of Oregon history, the themes and motifs of his fiction shifted toward the adventure, risks, and possibilities of economic development in a new land. The characters of his last novels are builders, developers, and contributors to an emerging civilization.

The two women of this novel clearly represent contrasting attitudes toward the frontier. Caroline Dance resists change and movement. She wants a quiet farm where she can be settled for life, away from town and close to nature. Lucy Overmire, on the other hand, is more curious and adventuresome, always wanting to know what is over the next hill. Stuart is drawn first to Caroline but ends up with Lucy. The women represent two forces in the development of the West: the settler and the adventurer, the force of pastoral agrarianism and the force of visionary ambition. This theme is reinforced in the portrayal of Clenchfield, Stuart's clerk in his mercantile business. Clenchfield is from England, and "the Old World had trained its children not to dare beyond their proper place. Clenchfield did not understand that America was all motion and change, that failure was never permanent unless a man deliberately made it so, that disaster was something to meet and forget and walk away from. America had no limits except those a man placed upon himself." This patriotic boosterism probably suited the mood of the country near the end of the war, but Haycox was not simply catering to nationalistic emotion: he genuinely subscribed to this view of America. His childhood in the West in the twilight of the frontier era, his being put on his own at an early age, his working hard and achieving success, his journey from selling newspapers on the street to owning a mansion in the hills above Portland—these things fostered his convictions about the opportunities available to those with dreams and determination. When in his last novels he turned from horse-opera formula to writing about his native region and attempting to express his deepest points of view, his heroes are venturers in opportunities provided by a new land— steamboats, stages, lumber, and grain mills. And his themes are variations of the statement about America just quoted from *Canyon Passage*.

Haycox's view of the western frontier was positive but not simplistic. He recognized that life in the West was just as conducive to failure as to success; it brought out the worst as well as the best in people. Character was the determining factor, and the West tested character in ways different from the East. Haycox maintained this conviction throughout his career. It is revealing, in this regard, that his first and last serialized novels, *Free Grass* and *Canyon Passage*, feature friends of the hero who are suited for the East but who go bad in the West. In *Free Grass* it is Lispenard. Reared in the graces of civilization and knowing right from wrong, he degenerates in the unrestrained environment of the frontier. In *Canyon Passage* it is George Camrose, who similarly degenerates into villainy. His friend Logan Stuart says of him, "In another kind of country he might have made the grade. Here, he lost out." Haycox's fiction is characterized by the recognition that if life in the West accentuated courage and integrity, it also magnified people's cowardice, laziness, and narrow-minded selfishness.

As a writer of serials, Haycox was at his peak in the mid-1940s. As one reviewer of *Canyon Passage* put it, "Mr. Haycox is a man who knows what he is doing, and that is all there is to it." But although he knew what he was doing, he was unsatisfied with what he was doing. He was compelled by a desire to abandon the magazine market and write novels freed from the conventions of the serial form.

The Novels

Haycox's letters to Thacher during the 1940s are filled with the turmoil of his artistic ambitions in tension with his uncertainties. He used Thacher as a sounding board for his near obsessive compulsion to change directions in his writing. In July of 1944 he told him, "I doubt if I write another straight western." He was not sure historical fiction was the answer, but that was the direction he was taking, constantly looking for some advance, some difference. He explained that for a long time he had thought he needed a definite and mature philosophy in order to write fiction of real quality. His thinking had been colored by this belief, and it had delayed his doing more substantial work. Now he was convinced that the belief was false, at least for him, because he could never be satisfied with any formula of life. Life is too "capricious, arbitrary, changeable" to be adequately encompassed in any systematic rational philosophy. Haycox believed that Emerson had been wrong in his idealism and Dreiser in his naturalism. He put aside the question of whether he might be a better writer if he had more positive convictions and concluded that "I shall have to write somewhat like the referee who follows the players and uses his whistle as little as possible. Of course my essential beliefs will condition my use of the whistle." He condensed those beliefs to a recognition of "an immense amount of beauty and glory and wonder in the world—in people"—combined with an awareness of an immense amount of tragedy and disillusionment, some of it self-inflicted, most of it not. All of this, as a writer, he observed with a good deal of compassion but also with the realization that the stream of life keeps moving and the individual is absorbed in the general current: "For a writer, I believe it is important to feel and to portray the full passion within Romeo and his girl friend; but also to portray them as they would have been at sixty—the ardor gone and their days concerned with indigestion and the social security check." He concluded the letter by repeating his new belief that a philosophy—a systematic explanation of life—was not essential: "What seems necessary is to have a good eye, some understanding—and follow the ball."[17] The truth is, he never escaped large philosophical concerns. Convincing himself that a definitive philosophy was unnecessary was just one way to fortify himself to breach those inner dikes that confined him to magazine fiction. He never gave up the notion that some kind of worldview is necessary for an author, and his next novels are obviously shaped by a distinct philosophy.

Haycox brought up the same matter in a letter of the following year, admitting to being in turmoil because the hunger to do better work had been particularly intense: "It has been a year of great dissatisfaction, of swinging all around the compass." He acknowledged apologetically that he had been sharing such "straining and heaving" with Thacher for a long time but described himself as "a very slow-maturing type. In fact it is apt to be a race between maturity and senescence." As it turned out, of course, cancer intervened in that race. At this point he was still troubled about the role of rational philosophy in creative writing; he distrusted the "literary geometry" of setting up a theme and then demonstrating it. He suspected that the core of the matter was his "unchangeable distrust of the human mind, or reason, or intellect, or rationalism, of the power of knowledge or of man's application of knowledge. I think I am a Know-Nothing, a barn-burner, a herd-jumper. I do have a considerable surface respect for facts. I respect history. I admire the man of learning and I know what discipline has gone into his search for it. . . . Yet I cannot be convinced that man is motivated in any great degree by reason. He will perhaps make reasoned decisions when there is no pressure on him; when pressure is upon him he will revert to the call of his tissues."[18] Probably behind his fretting over philosophical positions was his uncertainty about what constitutes serious literature. With the slight sense of inferiority natural to a writer who had been trained in the pulps, he suspected—even though he knew better—that writing first-class literature requires profound ideas. In these letters he is reassuring himself that is not so. His previously mentioned essay of the following year, "Writers: Dealers in Emotion," was another attempt to put this matter to rest.

Churning ambition is the common thread in his letters to Thacher: "I've got twenty novels on the shelf and that's about a lifetime's work for the average writer. It is not a bad record at all, but it does not represent more than half of me. It would be sad to leave only that for the record." And he didn't try to veil his ambition in the guise of pure artistic questing: "It isn't any of the impressive literature of artistic honesty, or the sweeping manifestos of literary purpose which impel me. There is really

only one reason why I want to do good work: it blisters me to think I'm
not at the top of this profession. That's scarcely an intellectual reason—
but it's the very same reason which animates most men who want to
push on." But the question was how it was to be done: "I know that I
have the old formula pretty well fixed in my nervous system, and that I
shall have to break it. Yet breaking an old formula is not enough. You
can break away from a formula; you cannot break away from form.
There must be form." This matter of form or method perplexed him. He
had been working more than 20 years in a standard story form. Could he
do distinctive new work in that form now or would the familiarity and
triteness of it take the edge off the new things he wanted to accomplish?
This perplexity made him feel like a beginner again. He said that the situation demonstrated what happens to writers from time to time:
"Tremendous unrests come upon us, and terrible uncertainties, and at
those times all the painfully acquired rules and the long established writing disciplines cease to mean anything. We look around us and assess the
work of various people who are considerably acclaimed and we do what
almost every amateur invariably does: we seek the key which will unlock
the puzzle. Well, of course, there's no key." Moreover, serial writing
allowed little room for experimenting. "Perhaps," he said, "I shall have
to forget about the serial market entirely in order to do what I wish. But
I shan't make that break until I am convinced I know what I am
doing."[19] The money reasons for being cautious were clear: he could
make $25,000 with a serial and $5,000 at most with a hardcover book.
He didn't live to see the full burgeoning of the paperback industry.

This was Haycox's unsettled state of mind when he wrote *Long Storm*,
a story set in Portland in 1862. Adam Musick is captain of a steamboat
that carries passengers and cargo up the Columbia. He is in competition
with a company that has a near monopoly on river traffic. But the real
villain is Floyd Ringrose, who, though the leader of a secret group of
Confederate sympathizers, is really seeking his own interests. Adam is
engaged to a woman who is socially conscious and afraid to give herself
wholly to him. A second woman understands him better, loves him
more, and eventually wins him. The conflict governing the plot is
Adam's need to temper his cynical fighting philosophy with kindness
and hope.

This narrative began as another *Post* serial, but after 30 pages Haycox
decided to make it the kind of novel he had been aiming for. He asked
Thacher to read the first draft before he made revisions, telling him,
"This story represents a break with what I have been doing. I propose to

continue in this manner until I have found the form and the substance which seems right. If this story has any novelistic possibilities I shall, in the revision, take out the serial vestiges still clinging to it. . . . If it has insufficient novel possibilities I propose to rewrite it into a serial—and try another experiment on another idea." He said he had sent a copy to his agent, whom he knew would encourage him to stick to his successful serial form. But he was prepared to discount that advice, for he was committed to change and intended to keep at it: "I cannot stick to the serial story and do what I wish to do. I've tried that, and find that the writing disciplines of 20 years' making hold me much too tight. I have got to break the old disciplines and set up a new group. You know that I have talked about this for many years, and have wanted to make the break for many years. It would have happened long ago if I'd known how to go about it. I'm not sure I yet know how to go about it, or that this story is the proper pattern for me; but anyhow it is a beginning." He impatiently asked Thacher to respond rapidly: "Time, as usual with me, is a-wastin'. I've only got another twenty years or so [in fact he had five]. There's much to be done." He conveyed the seriousness of his commitment by pointing out that in giving up this story as a serial he would be giving up $25,000. Then, with characteristic honesty and modesty, he added, "Well, really, that's not as noble as it sounds. After taxes it wouldn't be much more than $8,000—and in my present frame of mind money is not the thing I itch for."[20]

Neither Sanders nor Thacher liked the manuscript, but Haycox was tough enough to be objective about his work and desire objectivity from others. He conceded that the story was a failure as it stood: "This may seem like the surrendering of a thing fundamental to an author, which is complete faith in what he does. Had I complete faith in this story, I should argue with both of you, but I do not have that much faith." He agreed with Thacher that it is a serial-novel hybrid, but at this point he was uncertain whether to salvage it as a serial or to set it aside. He consoled himself with the thought that whatever he now did with it, it had been a breakthrough that he learned from. Three things about it drew his attention: "the hybridization it represents (in other words, we can't do it that way), the introverted way of presenting the people, and the romantic conception of the man-woman business."

As for the "introverted" method, he said that he had never liked it as a technique and had preferred telling the story by scenes and actions "rather than in the off-stage voice of the author." Yet he changed his mind in writing this story because he could not find a better way to present what he wanted to present. And he discovered that he enjoyed the method: it gave him a new sense of freedom. Now he was determined to continue using it: "Doing a story strictly in terms of people in action is not going to be enough for me. I have got to add some of the stream of consciousness business; only in that way can I create the final effects I seem to be after." What he was after were the undertones of a character engaged in internal struggle: "A scene has two dimensions. The gestures and reactions of the character supply something of a third dimension; but that is still not entirely enough. It is the soliloquy of a Hamlet which supplies the fourth dimension. In writing it is the man sitting down to go into his soliloquy without benefit of quotation marks which supplies the same effect." He realized that he had always used "a pinch of the introvert method" in his fiction, and it had given his stories whatever distinctive flavor they possessed. He now wanted to use the technique more extensively: "I have been a lean and economical writer for many years—and motion has been my primary rule." Now he believed that method doesn't allow the kind of power and massiveness he desired. He wanted something like Conrad's prodigality of description and Whitman's vast feeling.

Then he addressed the "man-woman business." His romanticism made him suspicious of the modern era's glandular, scientific explanation of sex that ignores its mystery—the longing and believing and projecting of ideals that go into a significant sexual relationship. He described science as "a magnificent skyscraper built by all sorts of careful plans and mathematical calculations; but below the bedrock of this skyscraper there's nothing but lava." He didn't underestimate "plain sex hunger. That is the principle of life working. But the principle of life cannot be plain hunger alone. It is a rare two human beings who can make much of a life out of that and nothing else." His conclusion: "Nope, I can't take my stand with the writers who go in for pure biological research. The longings of this race may start with sex and be powered by sex, but they leap beyond its moment and give it some meaning. The frustrations which occur in men and women are not only frustrations which come from physical inadequacy; they come also from imaginative inadequacy and spiritual inadequacy."[21] In his late fiction, particularly the last three novels, the emphasis on both the plain hunger of sex and its accompanying mystery is clearly apparent.

In *Long Storm* Haycox's distinctive romantic views of life and sex are intertwined. The novel portrays life as a process of disillusionment in collision with an eradicable impulse toward hope. As he told Thacher, "I think I shall try to say that the only permanence in this world, the only kind of way of achieving any fullness or roundness is in the love of a woman—whatever that love may be or may mean. Perhaps it is an illusion, but that cannot possibly matter. If it is an illusion, it is the most powerful of all, for as long as it may last."²² Christine Bold, who believes Haycox turned to naturalism in his later novels, says this one is filled with the language of social Darwinism (120). She is in large measure correct, but she minimizes the optimism so clearly apparent in his letters and in the endings of his novels. He used skepticism as an antagonist, not a protagonist. Even in this perhaps most skeptical of Haycox novels the hero reflects: "Hope was greater than anything. Maybe it had a meaning, maybe not; it made no difference, for hope was a force like the sun, and its presence was enough meaning for anybody." Later he chides himself for pessimistic thoughts: "He knew better. Whatever the disillusionment, no man could cease to hunt for what he wanted, or to hope for great things. Great things existed. It was men who destroyed them or made them seem hopeless." In capsule form, this is the worldview of the last novels. He expressed it directly in an essay published one year before his death: "We must believe there's a point to our lives and a point to our labors. If tomorrow science would show us definite proof that this earth was a clay ball flying meaningless through a meaningless space, and inhabited by creatures with no pattern and no purpose—if that evidence were to come to us, it would be necessary for us to reject it and somehow build a world and a universe in which we could believe."²³

There may be more of Haycox's inner life in *Long Storm* than in the novels preceding it. Indeed, the desire to get more of that inner life into his writing was one reason for his change in direction. The autobiographical connection is suggested when he wrote to Thacher: "As for Adam Musick—that introspective man—I have found a vehicle for him. Under another name he'll appear, someday but not this coming year, in a straight one-man story laid at the turn of the century in the Northwest." The story he then outlines is clearly autobiographical. But he never wrote it.

Despite Thacher's and Sanders's negative responses to the novel's first version, Haycox reworked it to remove the serial elements. Sanders submitted it to Little, Brown with the comment that it had not been written as a serial: "This definitely is not a book to be regarded as one of his regular Western stories; it is not likely that he will do more of those for he's growing." Raymond Everitt at Little, Brown liked it and said they would promote it as a major book: "We are delighted that Haycox is unlikely to go on with Westerns and you know I've had great faith for years in the fact that he will grow and do bigger and better novels."[24] Haycox was unsatisfied with the novel, and in returning the proofs he said that repairing the weaknesses would require rewriting the second half and be more work than the results would warrant: "This story represents an attempt to write both a novel and a serial. I have long known, theoretically, that such a straddle was impossible. This story demonstrated the impracticability in practical terms, yet it remains a passable story." As critical comment appeared, he was satisfied that the book was moving him away from the western category: "Thus, *Long Storm* has accomplished as much as I should hope for in the way of moving us in a new direction. The next novel I hope—and expect—will move us immeasurably farther."[25] *Long Storm* was selected by the Book League of America for its monthly selection, which meant sales of about 200,000 copies. It did not, however, appeal to paperback publishers: Dell turned it down in 1948 and Popular Library in 1949 on the grounds that its style was heavy, its action slow, and its subject not what the audience for westerns would expect.

The experiment of *Long Storm* pushed and pulled Haycox in several directions and strained his self-confidence. By May of 1946 he had recovered equilibrium. He wrote to Thacher, "I'm back in production after a two-year period of washing around. I think I must charge it up to artistic growth. That has a lovely, logical sound—and will do for an excuse. Still, there has been a change. I could not write some of the stories I wrote five years ago. I wish I could, since I enjoyed them so much. But my fingers will not trace the same patterns—and it would be foolish of me to try to force them into the old patterns."[26] But in fact he did attempt one more serial two years later—about transporting gold in eastern Oregon—but his heart wasn't in it. He kept saying to himself, "What the hell am I doing this for?"[27] Neither *Collier's* nor the *Post* wanted it. It appeared in condensed form in a single issue of *Esquire* in 1951 with the title "Head of the Mountain" and later in paperback editions. Part of being back in production, he told Thacher, was withdrawing from public activity. He had enjoyed it as a kind of revolt from his many years of strict writing discipline, as what he called a dose of salts to convince himself that he was not missing anything important by his devotion to writing.

Now his focus was on another novel, the logical follow-up to his experiments in *Long Storm*. He planned to involve his four main characters "in a set of emotions and circumstances as universal as I can make them, and told with as much truthfulness, and with as much literary excellence as I'm able." He was aiming for "the primitive, the robust, the elemental." He had slighted theme in the past, he said, but this time he had a theme he could honestly build on. He had come to believe that theme is more important for a novel than for a serial: "In fact I suspect that here lies the distinction between serial and novel. Action and plot to a great extent carry a serial along, but for a novel there must be an over-riding idea to supply the continuity and the motive power. This I seem to be discovering. As a matter of fact I rather imagine I shall write three or four of these damned things before I get any notion of where sure ground is." The title, *The Adventurers*, indicates that theme: "We are all adventurers; and some of us survive our adventures. Intelligence, planning, forethought, frugality, industry, worthiness—none of these things guarantee us a happy ending. Nothing guarantees us anything." But implied in this chance existence are two necessary qualities: courage and kindness.[28]

In his notes for the novel, under the heading "The Thought," Haycox wrote that the world is cruel and tests and breaks us: "Ambition wilts, faith goes, all the solid outer things in which we believed crumble; and our inner world is shaken. There seems no explanation or no law to cover the brutality which strikes the just and the unjust alike." Characteristically, however, this naturalistic view is balanced by a note under the heading "Slants": "Optimism should be stressed. These people are careless, full believers in things turning out all right; the free and easy ways of the west permit them to believe this." A combination of optimism and coarseness makes it possible for them to drive on and get things done: "A more sensitive people would not be suited to these surroundings." Under the heading "Feelings," he listed "pity, warmth, compassion, understanding, sympathy." This distinctive alloy of skepticism and hope, of cruelty and compassion, was the basic stuff of *Long Storm*, and so it was for *The Adventurers* and *The Earthbreakers*.

The Adventurers begins in 1865, with a shipwreck off the coast of Oregon. Three survivors—Mark Sheridan, George Revelwood, and Clara Dale—become fast friends and make their way to Portland. Sheridan, ambitious and capable, plans to enter the lumber business. Revelwood, a scoundrel with charm, plans to make money selling real estate and gold claims. Clara has inherited a house in Portland and plans to begin a new life there. A fourth main character, Katherine Morvain, is introduced when the survivors are washed ashore. She is the sturdy, constant pioneer woman, an elder daughter holding together a family with no mother and an ineffectual father. Clara, attracted to Sheridan but realizing he won't give himself fully to her, marries Revelwood and makes him miserable. Eventually Revelwood is hanged for shooting Clara's lover; Clara, in returning to San Francisco, throws herself overboard; and Sheridan, passing through the vicissitudes of adventuring in a developing land, is finally united with Katherine, who has lost most of her family. A well-drawn cast of supporting characters includes a suffragist whose husband is scorned by other men for supporting his wife, and a hearty Methodist preacher who is one of the most appealing characters Haycox ever created.

Haycox began *The Adventurers* with great enthusiasm. It would be twice as long as his usual narratives, receive more advance planning, and be written without a glance toward the serial market. It would lay the groundwork for his envisioned series of novels about Oregon.[29] At last he believed he knew what he wanted to write and how to do it. But doubts returned in the course of writing. He asked Thacher to read the manuscript, admitting that though he felt perfectly confident in the techniques of the serial, he was still perplexed about how to write a novel. He sent it to his agent—not for sale but for an opinion—telling him, "It is unfortunately not the novel I had in mind. It didn't pan out." Sanders was not encouraging, so Haycox replied, "Now then, it will go on the drydock for six months or a year. We shall forget about it as a marketable piece meanwhile. I plan to do a revision of it whenever I can crowd in the spare time."

The novel was another learning experience. Along with *Long Storm*, it taught him "to reject the whole romantic-realistic idea":

> In the ancient romantic-realistic classification system (which is an unreal concept at best) I have been on the romantic side. All my stories take the up note and all my characters are touched by a natural optimism, and by a certain gilding. My precise difficulty has been to inject realism into my people and to remove the Oliver Optic touch, the thought that God's got his eye on us and we're all right. So then I've been at war with myself, and the last two stories have been a struggle for some sort of firm ground for my people to stand on. I don't want soapy romance but I cannot abide the modern concept of realism which I think nothing better than a dreary accent on unimportant facts.

"Well," he told Sanders resignedly, "this is the second novel experiment. It hasn't gone so well, which is the penalty of experimentation. We shall have to keep at it."[30]

In July 1947 C. Raymond Everitt, his longtime friend and editor at Little, Brown, died. Angus Cameron took his place, assuring Haycox of his sympathetic interest in the plan for Oregon historical novels. Haycox, without mentioning *The Adventurers*, replied that he planned to continue in that direction: "I've broken from the straight-patterned western because it has become a skinny thing to me. I wish more meat on my story bones." Perhaps with *The Adventurers* in mind, he confessed the fault of going "a bit thick on think passages when I let my people have their heads": "I suppose the virus of the times has infected me—the virus of Significance. The cult nowadays is the Meaning behind the Meaning; in digging for better motivation for my characters I have sometimes fallen into that bear pit."[31] Here once again was his perennial uncertainty about balancing action and ideas—his desire to write serious literature in tension with his distaste for contemporary versions of it.

He had not yet given up entirely on *The Adventurers*. A year and a half later he sent it to Howard Cady for an opinion. Cady, once with Little, Brown, had moved to another company and was interested in recruiting Haycox. Cady's response to the manuscript was lukewarm, and Haycox decided to lay it aside, apparently for good. At least he had given up on the title, for "The Adventurers" is on the list of possible titles for *The Earthbreakers*. He seemed to have written the book off to experience and did not mention it in later correspondence. The manuscript, as Haycox left it, was eventually published in 1954 and chosen as a Literary Guild selection for January 1955.

Although *The Adventurers* failed to satisfy Haycox's hopes as a novelist independent of the magazine market, he remained determined to follow his ambition. In February 1949 he surprised Angus Cameron with a letter announcing his decision to change publishers. He said that *Canyon Passage* and *Long Storm* were the last novels he would do in the serial vein. During the intervening time he had been seeking a subject and method suitable for a serious novel: "The result is that I shall be embarking upon the first full novel this year, which represents a great deal of a gamble. To take as much risk from the gamble as possible I felt I needed the strongest possible guarantee in advance from a publisher; and since my name has so long been associated with sagebrush westerns I have also thought it necessary to make as clean a break as possible so that the new Haycox—if he turns out to be new—might have whatever promotional benefits accruing from a fresh start in a fresh wrapping." It is interesting that he made no mention of *The Adventurers*. The contract for *Long Storm* gave Little, Brown the option for his next novel. Haycox said that he considered the change in his writing program reason to alter the contract, but if Little, Brown insisted, they could have "a serial [*Head of the Mountain*] which I finished a couple of months ago to prove to myself that I couldn't write serials anymore." It did not sell, and he doubted they would want to publish it.[32] Why he did not offer *The Adventurers* is a puzzle. Apparently he considered it an experiment that Little, Brown did not need to know about.

The letter prompted immediate response from Cameron, who flew to Portland for two days to consult with Haycox. The result was a new contract for three novels about Oregon history: the first to be completed by February 1950, the second by February 1951, and the third by February 1953. A generous advance of $20,000 was provided and royalties of 15 percent. In addition, Haycox was assured that Little, Brown would work closely with him in this new endeavor, providing advice and critical response. Haycox and Cameron apparently discussed the nature of novel writing during their visit, for Cameron subsequently sent him two books on the subject—one of them E. M. Forster's *Aspects of the Novel*—and recommended two others.

Haycox's response to the Forster book reveals one of the principal challenges he encountered in attempting serious novels. He was interested in Forster's treatment of what Haycox considered the fundamental two ingredients of the novel: values vs. "and then-and then." He wrote, "That has been a problem I've wrestled with for five years, searching for the approach I wished to make on the full story. I tried the accent on values, diminishing the 'and then' business. But it won't work for me. My feeling is that the 'and then' is primary. It must be the novelist's first preoccupation to build his sheer story-telling frame; the rest, assuming he's a good writer, will find its way into the cracks and fissures of background and character, and so make roundness and/or significance." The writer concentrating on significance, he said, runs the risk of becoming a propagandist. A lifetime of writing adventure fiction obviously prompted the wrestling and shaped his conclusion.[33]

In April 1949 Haycox sent Cameron a long, detailed description of what was to become *The Earthbreakers*. This was the result of "the first four weeks' boiling," but of course considerable research had preceded the boiling. Haycox mentioned that he had seldom discussed stories with editors in advance of writing but that Little, Brown had "a healthy equity in this thing." His main concern was the "and then" stuff Forster seemed to downplay. He wanted this novel to have a driving, robust pace, a feeling of motion throughout. As for values and significance, they would develop out of the action. This consultation with Cameron from the very beginning suggests that Haycox needed to feel a sense of partnership and support in this project. He wrote regular progress reports to keep that sense alive. "Today I began the novel," he wrote on 27 June. On 28 July he reported 65 pages completed. Similar notifications were sent at pages 150, 227, 314, 354, 400, and 420. The first version of the novel was finished by the end of December 1949.

Set in 1845–46, *The Earthbreakers* opens as a wagon train of 400 people is preparing, after 2,000 miles and five months, to travel the last 90 miles into western Oregon by water through the gorge of the Columbia River. The November weather is wet, windy, and penetratingly cold. It breaks through one barrier after another inside a person until it reaches "that small center cell which housed the will to exist." The persistent and oppressive wet weather acts as a leitmotiv throughout the novel, reinforcing the fundamental theme of nature's indifference to human beings: "Man's dream of dignity was his own creation, not hers, and his suffering came of trying to make the dream real against the indifference of earth and sky to his individual fate." The five-month journey had taken its toll in "faith and flesh," and this last stretch is the "final wringing out of their endurance." The doctor for the party says, "In this gorge a lot of people will go beyond their breaking point—never quite be the same people again. Their free land's going to cost more than they think." He suggests they are running away from disillusionment with "the American notion we could start from nothing and become rich or get elected president." To admit the dream is false would be saying that hope is an illusion, so they have come to empty land for a fresh start, "hoping that what went wrong back East won't be wrong here." The novel takes them through the first year of settling, building, and planting.

It is the story of a community, but the principal character is Rice Burnett. Having been a soldier, a mountain man, and a jack-of-all-trades, he has come with the idea of settling down as a miller. Edna Lattimore attracts his basic sexual urges with her simple and direct sensuality; she is a sort of earth woman who frankly acknowledges physical desire and disdains any romantic illusions associated with sex. Katherine Gay is more refined and understands that sexual passion, important as it is, must be completed by qualities of mind, imagination, and spirit. Rice is seduced by Edna but eventually united with Katherine, who represents the best qualities of the pioneer woman. Cal Lockyear, another former mountain man, but one unsuited for accepting community living, is the principal antagonist. His individualistic, selfish lawlessness is a source of friction and violence.

Among the varied assortment of auxiliary characters is Bob Hawn, a mountain man living with his Indian wife in the area the pioneers intend to settle. He aids the new settlers, and in doing so alienates his wife, who senses she is losing him to white civilization. Burnett, Lockyear, and Hawn—three versions of the mountain man—function symbolically to express Haycox's probing examination of the dichotomies of wilderness-civilization; individualistic freedom-communal responsibility; and primitivism-progress.

Haycox's preoccupation with frontier gender conflict pervades the novel but is focused in the tension between Lot White, a fundamentalist preacher and male chauvinist, and Mrs. Millard, an outspoken pioneer feminist. White's pronouncements on women combine two conflicting myths common in the nineteenth century: that woman has a redemptive role in marriage and that woman leads man into evil. "God made you to haul the water and hew the wood. He made your flesh to close about man, he made you to be the tabernacle of man's faith. But the snake crept in and now the devil finds his best hidin' place right there in the creases of your body." Mrs. Millard is the kind of woman who can say to her husband after he has lost a leg in an accident: "Now you know what it's like to have other people do what you'd rather do yourself in your own way. Every woman born's in that position. Men doing this—men doing that. Always men. Woman does something. Man tears it down and does it over his way. How do you think we feel—made helpless when we don't want to be?"

With *The Earthbreakers*, Haycox had come a long way from pulp formulas, and he seemed more certain about the quandaries that troubled his middle years; for example, how important is a basic philosophy or worldview and how explicitly should it be expressed? Upon completing the novel, he wrote Cameron, "Modern writing—Hemingway—tends to convey a sense of discovery and search and confusion within people but to keep these things unexpressed—to let the reader's imagination do the rest. This avoids triteness and sometimes indicates depth and mystery to characters. It is the method of evoking rather than of open expression. But writing is something more than music and painting; it must not only evoke, it must state." He thought it a mistake to reduce the great range of the written word to the restrictions of the other arts. The writer must not demand too much of the reader's imagination: "Perhaps he might do so if he were writing strictly for the highly intuitive; but that's a very limited audience and not the audience which does this world's work. I grow leery of some of these pieces of modern fiction which require a bird dog, a compass, a map, and a set of critical reviews to become plausible."[34]

In the conception of this novel, Haycox seems to have found a worldview for his fiction. Somewhat like the naturalism of Frank Norris, it is a blending of realism and romanticism: the unblinking and amoral fidelity to detail of the former and the passion and drama of the latter. In a letter to Cameron, he stated the main idea he wished "to rub over the story—like a clove of garlic lightly rubbed over a piece of bread: There is no escape, no golden land, no security; it is a timeless illusion. We must sweat and cry. This will be in every future novel I write." He went on to explain that "since we must sweat and cry, we cannot refine out of ourselves the coarse, rough qualities by which people can alone endure the mud, the heat and the struggle." Had the people of his novel been more refined and sophisticated, he said, they would have failed. He included one refined couple for the very purpose of showing how their sensitivity handicapped them in that particular environment: "Nature cares nothing for the individual. The concept of human dignity and worth is something we invented to make a pattern for ourselves, without which we could not decently exist. Nature's interested only in carrying on a force, for some purpose we can't know. The individual is simply a vessel to carry that force on." Even the villain "had some principle below his evil which was beyond the classification of good and evil; it was the force with which he was endowed, amoral and too powerful for him."[35]

In a letter to Thacher, Haycox explained how gender fits into this scheme: "In the field of the individual: Woman is the constant, the changeless, the stronger. She is the field of force. Man's the dreamer, the restless and changeable one, the weaker. He, drifting along the edges of the field of force, is pulled into it. In the social order man is given dominance; in the order of nature woman is dominant."[36] In order to convey this point, Haycox treated the sexual scenes more explicitly than he had ever done before. This degree of frankness was too much for the London publisher, Hodder & Stoughton, who had published many of Haycox's previous novels. They agreed to publish *The Earthbreakers* but backed out of the contract when they found parts of the novel too sexually explicit. Similarly, Little, Brown's agent for arranging paperback publication reported in May 1952 that he was having no luck with the novel "because of its frankness in spots."[37]

The female aspect of the novel was of principal importance to Haycox. In sending the manuscript to Cameron to read, he said, "Some woman in this present story—don't know which one yet, but possibly Katherine, is going to appear in the next ones; she will be a continuing character right through until the century turns. I should like to develop her as a woman who has faced most of the hard situations of living through most of the stages of life."[38] In revising the manuscript, his principal concern was strengthening and expanding the character of Katherine. Cameron himself recognized the central role of women in this book and up until just months before publication was trying to bring "woman" into the title. He finally asked Haycox's widow to choose between "The Earthbreakers" and "The Earth Is a Woman." She thought her husband had been satisfied with the former.[39]

Haycox considered the novel "not a march of destiny story, or a triumph of virtue over evil, or a thesis on human happiness." But along with his naturalistic view he wanted to portray "the fraternity and survival value of the human race. I don't want a pollyanna story. Can't abide them. But I want a robust counter note for the prevailing wringing of hands we're going through now." He thought we have seen certain kinds of progress since the pioneer era but that we have also arrived at uncertainty, pessimism, and a lack of faith in our more vital qualities as humans: "I do not in the story suggest a return to the primitive or the 'natural man.' I only suggest a greater accent on our robust qualities—the direct action, the fresh flavor."[40] His admiration for the personal strength and confident direct action he associated with the western character was a constant in his temperament and is obvious in his fiction from beginning to end.

The Earthbreakers is not a western but a novel about the West. And it is not as much about the West in terms of action as it is about the meaning of the opening of the West for American culture. That meaning is examined with considerable penetration. Much is called into question for critique: the motivations behind pioneering; the gender and marriage relations created by the frontier; the romantic freedom and individualism of the mountain man; the encounter with Indians; the American dream; and the large issues of moral justice and the efficacy of religious belief.

Thacher described reading the manuscript of *The Earthbreakers* in this way: "I read it with growing delight, then with amazement, and finally with the jubilant sense of vicarious triumph. For in *The Earthbreakers* I was convinced that Erny had finally succeeded in doing what, frankly, I had long doubted he would be able to do: he had broken with his past and freed himself from the shackles which he himself had so sedulously forged through the long years." Cameron, in sharing his response to the novel with Thacher, said that he, too, had encouraged Haycox to write the books he really wanted to write and had tried to convince him that the difference between his westerns and the novels he wanted to write "lay in his willingness to expose not only what he knew about other people, but chiefly, what he knew about himself. He finally came to accept this view and, in fact, we discussed his characterization in *The Earthbreakers* with the full knowledge that a good many of the characteristics, both good and bad, which he found in the people were not characteristics of people Erny Haycox had known, but of Erny himself. His fear of exposing himself was finally overcome, I believe."[41]

Haycox was tired after completing the first version of the novel. "Beginning in effect a new career after an old one is not an easy business," he told Cameron. Yet in sending his editor the manuscript he was already enthusiastically describing the next novel, which was to pick up the thread of Oregon history in 1855.[42] And when Cameron provided suggestions for revising *The Earthbreakers*, Haycox responded in detail to each point and eagerly began the task of rewriting. Then on 29 April he wrote Cameron, "I got about 100 pages of the novel revised when I came down with a case of jaundice; so now I'm in bed, and will remain in bed for another week, and that will delay the completion of the revise by damned near a month." This was followed by a telegram from Jill on 18 May: "Erny had a cancerous tumor removed yesterday the doctors say he has an excellent chance." Haycox confronted the situation with courage and his usual self-effacement, assuring Cameron on 31 May that he considered himself "a functioning LB author." But his health continued to fail until his death four and a half months later, on 14 October 1950. The editors at Little, Brown completed the revisions along the lines Haycox had begun, and the novel was published in January 1952.

Conclusion

Any final estimation of Ernest Haycox must confront this question: Was he a failed serious novelist or a masterful writer of romantic adventure? Because his career evolved from pulps through slicks to books selected by literary clubs, and because he was ambitious until the end of his life to write something different and better, those evaluating his achievement tend to emphasize how close he came to writing "good" literature. And they suggest that had he lived longer he might have come even closer. According to this view, which seems supported by Haycox's own statements, his novels fell short of quality to the degree that they retained conventional elements of action adventure. In other words, he might have been a fine novelist if he had fully purged himself of western formulas.

This view seems natural and reasonable, but its self-evidence is actually based on the tastes and cultural expectations of a particular age. For most of our century, serious literature has been sharply distinguished from popular literature, the former being characterized by its best examples and the latter by its worst. This distinction has produced generalizations that are true and useful to a certain extent, but that are false and unfair applied to particular cases. The very imprecision of such terms as *serious* and *popular* suggests how questionable the distinction is. As Cynthia S. Hamilton argues in her study of the western and hard-boiled detective genres, "The hierarchical notion of culture is laden with preconceptions about the inherent limitations of formula."[1] High art is defined as an individual achievement, popular art as a social manifestation. The serious novelist is assumed to be more concerned with subject than with audience, with creative vision than with conventions. Quality novels are supposed to challenge and disturb readers, whereas popular novels merely offer confirmation and reassurance. Unfortunately, considering the popular novel to be different by nature from the serious one has the consequence of making it something other than a work of art. If popular literature is to be condemned, it must not be because it is not literature. Westerns use conventions, but so does high art. The issue should not be the limitations of conventions in themselves but the degree of skill and imagination with which they are used. Formula fiction is not a special case outside the pale of literary art; writing it well

126

requires the same artistic skills needed for any successful fiction. The level of artistry varies greatly within popular forms, and the relation between popular and serious forms is a continuum without sharp demarcations. Moreover, formulas are not static and lifeless, incapable of imaginative application and modification. Magazine fiction in Haycox's era was certainly shaped by the market, but the process of shaping was not as simple or irresistible or uniformly deleterious as is generally assumed. Editors were never completely certain what would appeal to readers, and their rein on the imaginations of writers—particularly the better ones—was never inflexibly firm.

It may be, in fact, that the marketplace had a more unfortunate effect on critics of the western than on the fiction itself. Critics have accepted the western as a market-defined category, mindlessly lumping together all levels of artistry within it and strictly applying stereotypes that discourage fresh and fair examination of individual authors. Wallace Stegner notes that the western—"horse opera" he calls the genre, echoing DeVoto—has been studied in considerable detail but acknowledges that critics rarely approach it from the near (or literary) side: "They mount it from the right, like Indians, and ride it hard as myth, as folklore, as a part of the history of ideas, or as a demonstration of Freudian or Jungian psychology. I don't recall ever seeing a Western discussed for its original social or psychological insights, for the complexity or depth of its characters, for its poetic evocativeness, for its narrative techniques, or for its prose style. It wouldn't pay to do it, for a Western is not a unique performance but a representative one" (Stegner, 187). This last sentence repeats the sentiment of DeVoto, whom Stegner greatly admired. There is truth here, but the statement illustrates that even a perceptive critic with western sympathies can be distracted by stereotypes from recognizing the possibility that a particular writer of westerns might merit being approached from the literary side. Haycox's fiction at its best moves from stereotypes to art and merits literary analysis. The characters, even those briefly mentioned, have imaginative substance, a kind of fictive flesh and bone. They combine weaknesses along with strengths and are psychologically interesting. In short, they are de-mythed. The fictional experience is plausibly grounded in the history of a time and evokes a vivid sense of place. And the environment is not mere picturesque backdrop; its influence on human action and character is manifest. Saul Bellow once said that a writer "should write clearly, take a moral view of his subject, and be capable of giving the most intense attention to his subject and characters." Haycox meets these admirably simple standards.

If we set aside the notion of an unbridgeable chasm separating popular and serious literature, and if we recognize that heroism and a certain element of melodrama have played a significant role in the best literature since that of the Greeks, then perhaps we can better appreciate Haycox for what he did accomplish rather than for how nearly he approximated the esthetic preferences of a particular age. And this appreciation will increase if we resist the fashion of lumping all westerns together and accounting for them with one sociological theory, as Jane Tompkins does in *West of Everything*: "For when you read a Western novel or watch a Western movie on television, you are in the same world no matter what the medium: the hero is the same, the story line is the same, the setting, the values, the actions are the same." And she accounts for this monolithic world in this way: "The Western doesn't have anything to do with the West as such. It isn't about the encounter between civilization and the frontier. It is about men's fear of losing their mastery, and hence their identity, both of which the Western tirelessly reinvents."[2] The nature and scope of Haycox's fiction give the lie to such generalizations. Haycox was like other popular Western writers, but he was also different in significant ways—ways involving subjects, themes, literary skill, psychological insight, and moral vision.

Haycox's achievement is also better understood if we acknowledge that popular literature has purpose and value in its own right. As Ross Macdonald points out, "Popular art is the form in which a culture comes to be known by most of its members. It is the carrier and guardian of the spoken language. A book which can be read by everyone, a convention which is widely used and understood in all its variations, holds a civilization together as nothing else can. It reaffirms our values as they change, and dramatizes the conflicts of those values."[3] Joseph Conrad expresses a similar view in his novel *Chance*: "We are the creatures of our light literature much more than is generally suspected in a world which prides itself on being scientific and practical, and in possession of incontrovertible theories."[4] And G. K. Chesterton was another who defended sensational novels, claiming they were the "most moral" part of modern fiction and asserting that "any literature that represents our life as dangerous and startling is truer than any literature that represents it as dubious and languid. For life is a fight and is not a conversation."[5] Because romantic adventure fiction serves a significant purpose and supplies literary pleasure for a large readership, we ought to concern ourselves with delineating its levels of artistic quality and celebrating the achievements of its finest authors. From this perspective, Haycox's fiction fares well.

It does not fare well, however, when Haycox is simplistically viewed as a willing prisoner of popular demand, yielding to the blandishments of money in exchange for serving the emotional needs of his readers, thus denying himself the freedom that he needed in order to treat his subject more thoughtfully. Readers have a variety of emotional needs, including those fulfilled by heroic adventure. The western hero is necessarily a mythic figure. We do not really believe in him, but at the same time we would not have him step out of his conventionalized background. The fact that he is larger than life does not diminish his power but enlarges it. He has, after all, his own kind of relevance. For over a century, the myth has satisfied some too easily and uncritically and troubled others too excessively and hypercritically; but it has survived both responses. It has survived shameless exploitation, trivialization, and distortion on the one hand and charges of racism, sexism, and imperialism on the other. It has endured in part because it embodies simultaneously elements of national identity and elements of universal aspiration. And its serviceability apparently has not yet ended. Certainly in Haycox's era it served the emotional needs of an enormous readership. Restrained as he was by market demands, Haycox, as we have seen, was no mere prisoner. Besides having some room for artistic development and thoughtful expression, he enjoyed the freedom provided by his sincere respect for the western ethos he saw underlying the conventions. Besides, all writers are under some kinds of limitations and restraints. Why single out the popular market as the most deplorable of them?

It may be possible, after all, for a writer to prostitute himself or herself up as well as down. Haycox recognized the temptation of becoming a pulp hack, but he also viewed conforming to certain trends in serious literature as an equally enticing but dangerous temptation. He recognized a sort of formula of formlessness in what was considered the serious literature of his time, a straining for "Significance." "I think that as rigid in its way as the formula of action and happy ending," he wrote Thacher. "Some of the best stories in America come from this group; and some of the most pointless and vacillating tales come from it. To avoid the pattern of the obvious the writers in this group fall into the pattern of dark and dismal obscurity."[6]

C. S. Lewis remarked in 1936 that the power of painting virtue convincingly was absolutely unknown in his generation.[7] Had he known Haycox's work, he might have modified that assertion, for Haycox portrayed the heroic virtues as convincingly as anyone in that generation. His work belies the common notion that all westerns are morally naive or trite. Lionel Trilling observed that "All novelists deal with morality, but not all novelists, or even all good novelists, are concerned with moral realism, which is not the awareness of morality itself but of the contradictions, paradoxes and dangers of living the moral life."[8] Haycox's hero rises above the commonplace western protagonist because his moral code, without ceasing to be compelling, is seen also to be conflicted and imperfect. He displays a moral ambiguity that deepens our image of him and saves him from absurdity. The ambiguity derives from the fact that, whatever his justification, he is a killer of men. His victory can never be complete because even necessary violence leaves its mark. He escapes with his life but has been forced to the limits of his moral ideas. The mature sense of limitation and unavoidable guilt is what prompts his melancholy. Haycox's moral vision encompasses "the geography of loneliness, the ecstasy of freedom threatened by the imminence of doom, the dream of innocence become the nightmare of guilt, the hope of heroism fraught with the prospect of failure and the dwarfness of spirit."[9]

A final argument for the proposition that Haycox warrants consideration on his literary merits despite the fact that he wrote popular fiction concerns the issue of violence. The violence of commonplace westerns is often gratuitous and excessive, and this is particularly true of recent film versions. But violence was never an end in itself for Haycox; it was never the point of his stories, and he never used more than was necessary to express the human conflicts that were the point of his stories. Violence in his fiction is an understood violence—violence perceived in its inevitability and value as well as in its senselessness and waste. The drama is one of self-restraint: the moment of violence must come in its own time and according to its special laws. Unlike writers of lower-grade westerns, Haycox used guns with attention to motive and the human meanings to be realized through violence. His primary concern was not gunfire and fistfights but a certain image of human character and struggle that reveals itself most clearly in such violence.

Current intellectual opinion refuses to acknowledge any value in violence. This refusal is a virtue, but like many virtues it involves a degree of willful blindness and hypocrisy; and it sometimes, paradoxically, invites further violence. We train ourselves to be shocked or bored by cultural images of violence, but not to confront them. In serious art physical heroism seems now a little embarrassing and childish. In the popular media it is violent, self-indulgent, and pointless. And in the criticism of popular culture, often done by educated observers under the illusion that they have nothing at stake in the portrayal of violence, the presence of images of violence is often assumed to be in itself sufficient ground for condemnation. Because we have refused to recognize the value of violence and the value of a kind of heroism that comes to grips with it in a meaningful way, violence is left in the hands of the least responsible and most cynically exploitative producers of books, television, films, and comic books. The refusal to grapple with the full nature of violence—its uses as well as abuses—and instead condemn it categorically on the one hand and glorify it and indulge our lowest instincts with it on the other has freed violence from moral restraints. Haycox's fiction explores human violence as only skillful literary art can do, weighing its inevitability, its contradictions, and its demands for mature moral behavior.

Notes and References

Preface

    1. *Approaches to Writing*, 2d ed. (Middleton, Conn.: Wesleyan University Press, 1988), 32.

Chapter One

    1. "Phaethon on Gunsmoke Trail," *Harpers,* October 1954, 14, 16.

    2. Jill Marie Haycox, introduction to *The Earthbreakers,* by Ernest Haycox (Boston: Gregg Press, 1979), ix; hereafter cited in text.

    3. "Writing Offbeat Westerns," *Chronicles*, August 1991, 20–23.

    4. See, for example, Russell Nye, *The Unembarrassed Muse: The Popular Arts in America* (New York: Dial Press, 1970), 303; Christine Bold, *Selling the Wild West: Popular Western Fiction, 1860 to 1960* (Bloomington: Indiana University Press, 1987), 76; and John A. Dinan, *The Pulp Western: A Popular History of the Western Fiction Magazine in America* (San Bernardino, Calif.: Borgo Press, 1983), 82.

    5. "Letter to a Graduate Student," *Roundup* 12 (November 1965): 6.

    6. *Short Stories*, 14 May 1930. Reprinted in *Lone Rider* (New York: Popular Library, 1959).

    7. "The West of Haycox Westerns," *Call Number* 25 (Fall 1963–Spring 1964): 29.

    8. "Ernest Haycox: An Appreciation," *Call Number* 25 (Fall 1963–Spring 1964): 3.

    9. *The Mythic West in Twentieth-Century America* (Lawrence: University Press of Kansas, 1986), 167.

    10. Review of *Riders West, Boston Transcript*, 21 July 1934.

    11. "Ernest Hemingway's Grace under Pressure: The Western Code," *Pacific Historical Review* 45 (1976): 430.

    12. *New York Herald-Tribune Book Review,* 8 October 1950, 4.

    13. "Ernest Haycox: A Study in Style," *Roundup* 21 (February 1973): 2.

    14. "The Western and Ernest Haycox," *Prairie Schooner* 26 (1952): 179.

    15. Haycox to Angus Cameron, 3 January 1950, Haycox Family Papers.

    16. In *Northwest Harvest*, ed. V. L. O. Chittick (New York: Macmillan, 1948), 39–51.

    17. Richard W. Etulain, "The Literary Career of a Western Writer: Ernest Haycox, 1899–1950," Ph.D. diss. (University of Oregon), 1966, 34; hereafter cited in text.

18. Robert Ormond Case to W. F. G. Thacher, 5 February 1952, Haycox Collection.

19. Stuart Holbrook, *The Story of American Railroads* (1947; New York: American Legacy Press, 1981), 404–405.

20. Reed College admissions records, Haycox Collection.

21. "Soldiering: First Impressions and Later Corrections," *The Cardinal* 20 (June 1917): 58.

22. "Back from the Border," *The Cardinal* 20 (October 1916): 31–33; "Soldiering: First Impressions and Later Corrections," 31–33.

23. Haycox to Mary Haycox, 29 June 1916, Haycox Collection.

24. Reed College registration form, 14 October 1919, Reed College Records, Haycox Collection; Haycox to Arnold Gates, 1 July 1942, Haycox Collection.

25. "Application for Admission," September 1919, Reed College Records, Haycox Collection.

26. *The Writer* 34 (September 1922): 129–30.

27. *Emerald*, 6 October 1921.

28. "Portland Author Has Story in *Sunday Journal*," Portland *Oregon Journal*, 20 February 1936, 22.

29. Thacher to Charles R. Morse, 5 December 1929, Thacher Papers, University of Oregon.

30. Thacher to Case, 25 May 1936, Thacher Papers, University of Oregon.

31. W. F. G. Thacher, "Teaching Short-Story Writing in the Colleges," *Author and Journalist* 9 (April 1924): 17.

32. Thacher to Giles L. French, 8 October 1924, Eric Allen Papers, University of Oregon.

33. Wallace S. Wharton, "Writing a Working Craft," *Oregon Sunday Journal*, 31 March 1935, 9. Haycox actually received $25 for the story according to Etulain (Etulain 1966, 63).

34. Haycox Collection, University of Oregon.

35. Wetjen to John Hawkins, [10 February 1938], Hawkins Papers, University of Oregon.

36. "A Persistent Writer's Success," *The Writer* 34 (September 1922): 130.

37. Haycox to Charles Alexander, August [1922], Alexander Papers, University of Oregon.

38. Haycox to Charles Alexander, 11 March 1923, Alexander Papers, University of Oregon.

39. Haycox to Thacher, 21 June 1934, Haycox Collection.

40. Haycox to Thacher, [1931–32], Haycox Collection.

Chapter Two

1. "A Persistent Writer's Success," 129.

2. Arthur Larson, "Writing Vital Passion for Ernest Haycox," *Oregonian,* 11 May 1969; hereafter cited in text.

3. Haycox to Arthur B. Epperson, 23 February 1930, Haycox Collection.

4. Haycox to Angus Cameron, 3 January 1950, Little, Brown Archives.

5. Wharton, "Writing a Working Craft," 9; hereafter cited in text.

6. W. F. G. Thacher, "Oregon Writers I Have Known," typescript lecture in the Haycox Collection. At the time of Haycox's death, Blackwell told his widow in a letter, "I am proud that, if not *the* first, I was *among* the first to recognize Ernest's great ability, and also, his sterling character." Quoted in Clark Brooker, "Ten Thousand Stories Untold," *Roundup* 21 (October 1973): 13.

7. Dinan, *The Pulp Western,* 5; hereafter cited in text.

8. Irving Harlow Hart, "The Most Popular Authors of Fiction in the Post-War Period, 1919–1926," *Publishers Weekly*, 12 March 1927, 1045–53.

9. Cynthia S. Hamilton, *Western and Hard-Boiled Detective Fiction in America: From High Noon to Midnight* (Iowa City: University of Iowa Press, 1987), 56; hereafter cited in text.

10. Robert Ormond Case, "The Difference Is Real People, *Roundup* 6 (October 1958): 3; hereafter cited in text.

11. Bound rejection letters in the Haycox Collection.

12. John Schoolcrift, ed., *The Notebooks and Poems of Max Brand* (New York: Dodd, Mead, 1957), 39.

13. Bold, *Selling the Wild West,* 93; hereafter cited in text.

14. "The Golden Age of Pulps," *Atlantic,* July 1961, 59.

15. "A Man's Life," *The Cardinal* 20 (December 1916): 31.

16. The *Oxford English Dictionary* dates the first use of "western" as a noun as late as 1930. Cynthia S. Hamilton found an earlier use in an advertisement in the 15 October 1927 issue of *Saturday Review.* It took a while for the term to catch on. An advertisement for Haycox's *Whispering Range* in December 1930 said, "Sell this popular new 'WESTERN.'" The capitalization and quotation marks suggest that the term was still uncommon. Haycox was just beginning to publish novels when the term was becoming current.

17. "Budd Dabbles in Homesteads," *Western Story,* 1 November 1924, 97.

18. Illustrated by Carl Kidwell (New York: Criterion, 1954).

19. Haycox to Arnold Gates, 5 October 1938, Haycox Collection.

20. See Northrop Frye, *Anatomy of Criticism* (Princeton, N.J.: Princeton University Press, 1957; repr., New York: Athenaeum, 1965), 101; Philip Rahv, "The Dark Lady of Salem," in *Essays on Literature and Politics, 1932–1972,* eds. Arabel J. Porter and Andrew J. Dvosin (Boston: Houghton Mifflin, 1978).

21. *Short Stories,* 10 January 1928, collected in *Trigger Trio* (New York: Ace Books, 1966).

22. Most of these are novelettes: "Bound South" (*Short Stories,* 10 March 1928); "A Municipal Feud" (*Short Stories,* 10 May 1928); "Invitation by Bullet" (*Short Stories,* 25 April 1929; collected in *Vengeance Trail* [New York: Popular Library, 1955]); "Night Raid" (*Frontier,* April 1929; collected in *Brand Fires on*

the Ridge [New York: Monarch Books, 1959]); "Contention—Two Miles Ahead" (*Short Stories,* 25 September 1929; collected in *Powder Smoke* [New York: Avon, 1966]); "Five Hard Men" (*Short Stories,* 10 November 1929; collected in *Gun Talk* [New York: Popular Library, 1956]); "The Trail of the Barefoot Pony" (*Short Stories,* 25 September 1929; collected in *Secret River* [New York: Popular Library, 1955]); "The Killers" (*Short Stories,* 10 July 1930; collected in *Brand Fires on the Ridge* [New York: Pinnacle Books, 1990]).

23. Haycox to Thacher, 1 February 1929, Haycox Collection.
24. Ibid.
25. Haycox to Alexander, 15 February 1929; Charles Alexander Papers, University of Oregon.
26. *The Land of Forgotten Men* (New York: A. L. Burt, 1923), 301.
27. Haycox to Alexander, 25 March [1931], Charles Alexander Papers, University of Oregon.

Chapter Three

1. Wetjen to Hawkins, [10 February 1938], Hawkins Papers, University of Oregon.
2. Hickman Powell, *"Collier's,"* Scribners Magazine, May 1939, 20; Norman Vogt, *"Collier's,"* in *American Mass-Market Magazines,* eds. Alan and Barbara Nourie (New York: Greenwood Press, 1990), 56.
3. Haycox to Epperson, 15 May 1931, Haycox Papers, Oregon State Historical Society Library, Portland.
4. John Chord, "Certain Dedications," Haycox Collection.
5. Thacher, "Oregon Writers I Have Known."
6. Haycox to Thacher, [1932], Haycox Collection.
7. *Status Rerum: A Manifesto upon the Present Condition of Northwestern Literature* (The Dalles: privately printed [1927]).
8. Jill Haycox to Stanley Salmen, 13 February 1952, Little, Brown Archives.
9. Haycox to Thacher, 19 February [1937], Haycox Collection.
10. Haycox to Epperson, 8 September 1932, Haycox Papers.
11. Haycox to Thacher, 31 July 1944, Haycox Collection.
12. Haycox to Ray Everitt, 22 March 1939, Little, Brown Archives.
13. James Fargo, "The Western and Ernest Haycox," *Prairie Schooner* 26 (1952): 180 (hereafter cited in text); anonymous, "Fact Sheet—Ernest J. Haycox," Oregon State Historical Society Library, Portland.
14. Ernest Haycox, Jr., introduction to *Bugles in the Afternoon,* by Ernest Haycox (Boston: Gregg Press, 1978), ix–x; hereafter cited in text.
15. Haycox to Harold G. Merriam, 9 July 1932, Haycox Collection.
16. Haycox to Thacher [December 1932], Haycox Collection.
17. Haycox to Epperson, 1 February [1931], Haycox Collection.
18. Haycox to Kenneth Littauer, 12 January 1935, *Collier's* Papers, New York Public Library.

19. Haycox to Merriam, 20 July 1932, Haycox Collection.

20. "Writers: Dealers in Emotion," *Library Journal*, 15 February 1946, 248.

21. Haycox to Thacher, 23 March 1938, Haycox Collection.

22. Haycox to Thacher, [December 1934], Haycox Collection.

23. Haycox to Thacher, 21 June 1934, Haycox Collection.

24. Haycox to Merriam, 9 July 1932, Haycox Collection.

25. Wallace Stegner, *The Sound of Mountain Water* (New York: E. P. Dutton, 1980), 184; hereafter cited in text.

26. Haycox to Thacher, 30 November [1934], Haycox Collection.

27. "Down These Streets a Mean Man Must Go," in *Self-Portrait: Ceaselessly into the Past* (Santa Barbara, Calif.: Capra Press, 1981), 7.

28. "Archer at Large," in *Self-Portrait*, 30.

29. "Recapture," *Redbook*, June 1934.

30. Haycox to Littauer, 3 May 1938, *Collier's* Papers, New York Public Library.

31. *Oregon Daily Journal*, 20 February 1936.

32. Haycox to Thacher, [December 1934], Haycox Collection.

33. "Their Own Lights," 7 October 1933; "The Man with the Smoke Gray Eyes," 1 December 1934; "Against the Mob," 12 January 1935; "Once and for All," 16 November 1935; and "Proud People," 23 May 1936.

34. "The Man with the Smoke Gray Eyes," 1 December 1934.

35. "Against the Mob," 12 January 1935.

36. Brooker, "Ten Thousand Stories Untold," 12.

37. David Cary, *Cowboy Culture: A Saga of Five Centuries* (Lawrence: University of Kansas Press, 1989), 107.

Chapter Four

1. Littauer to Haycox, 23 March 1938, *Collier's* Collection.

2. Haycox to Thacher, [December 1934], Haycox Collection.

3. Chenery to Haycox, 25 March 1937, *Collier's* Collection.

4. Chenery to Haycox, 7 October 1937, *Collier's* Collection.

5. Haycox to Chenery, 1 April 1938, *Collier's* Collection.

6. Littauer to Haycox, 31 December 1937, *Collier's* Collection.

7. Littauer to Sanders, 21 February 1939, *Collier's* Collection.

8. For a survey of Haycox's fiction during these years, see Richard Etulain, "Ernest Haycox: The Historical Western, 1937–43," *South Dakota Review* 5 (1967): 35–54.

9. Harold Brainerd Hersey, *Pulpwood Editor* (Westport, Conn.: Greenwood Press, 1937), 165.

10. Donald D. Walker provides a trenchant critique of DeVoto's theory of the western in *Clio's Cowboys: Studies in the Historiography of the Cattle Trade* (Lincoln: University of Nebraska Press, 1981) and in a series of articles in a newsletter printed at the University of Utah, *The Possible Sack* 2 (July 1971):

1–7, 2 (August 1971): 6–8, and 3 (March 1972): 14–18. Walker argues that DeVoto is more historian than literary critic and that his focus on historical accuracy causes him to ignore imaginative coherence; consequently, historical accuracy displaces artistic effect as a desideratum. Walker's theory is much more congenial than is DeVoto's to Haycox's aims and achievements.

11.   Bernard DeVoto, *Minority Report* (Boston: Little, Brown, 1940), 89.

12.   Sanders quotes Haycox's letter in a letter to Littauer, 4 May 1937, *Collier's* Collection.

13.   Chenery to Haycox, 14 May 1937, *Collier's* Collection.

14.   Haycox to Thacher, 23 March 1938, Haycox Collection.

15.   Haycox to Littauer, 25 April 1938, *Collier's* Collection.

16.   *The Popular Book: A History of America's Literary Trade* (New York: Oxford University Press, 1950), 261.

17.   Lyle Downing, "Ernest Haycox: Police Reporter to Famous Fictioner," *Oregonian,* 24 October 1943, 2.

18.   Haycox to Littauer, 7 July 1938, *Collier's* Collection.

19.   Richard L. Neuberger, review of *The Adventurers, New York Times Book Review,* 2 January 1955, 5.

20.   Haycox to Epperson, 25 August [1932], Haycox Collection.

21.   Haycox to Epperson, 26 April [?], Haycox Collection.

22.   Haycox to Fred [?], 22 January 1945, Haycox Collection.

23.   Haycox to Gates, 2 February 1938, Haycox Collection.

24.   "The Ernest Haycox Memorial Library," *The Call Number* 25 (Fall–Spring 1964): 29.

25.   Sanders to Littauer, 12 July 1936, *Collier's* Collection.

26.   Haycox to Littauer, 22 June 1935, *Collier's* Collection.

27.   "The Petrified West and the Writer," in *Western Writing,* ed. Gerald W. Haslam (Albuquerque: University of New Mexico Press, 1974), 145.

28.   "The Historical Novel," in *Western Writing,* 54.

29.   Haycox to Littauer, 29 March 1938, *Collier's* Collection.

30.   "Can the Western Tell What Happens?" in *Critical Essays on the Western American Novel,* ed. William T. Pilkington (Boston: G. K. Hall, 1980), 96.

31.   Haycox to Thacher [December or January 1934–35], Haycox Collection.

32.   Haycox to Thacher, 2 February 1937, Haycox Collection.

33.   Haycox to Thacher, 19 February [1937], Haycox Collection.

34.   Haycox to Thacher [December 1945 or 1946], Haycox Collection.

35.   "Sir Walter, Excepting . . . ," *Writer's Digest,* February 1942, 12; "Writers: Dealers in Emotion," 248.

36.   Haycox to Thacher [February 1937], Haycox Collection.

37.   Haycox to Littauer, 1 February 1938, *Collier's* Collection.

38.   Littauer to Haycox, 8 February 1938, *Collier's* Collection.

39.   Davenport to Haycox, 24 February 1938, *Collier's* Collection.

40. Littauer to Haycox, 31 January 1939, and Haycox to Littauer, 6 February 1939, *Collier's* Collection.

41. Chenery to Haycox, 14 July 1938 and 4 August 1938, *Collier's* Collection.

42. Haycox to Chenery, 8 August 1938, *Collier's* Collection.

43. Haycox to Littauer, 3 May 1939, *Collier's* Collection.

44. Littauer to Haycox, 2 August 1939, *Collier's* Collection.

45. Haycox to Littauer, 1 September 1939 and 11 January 1939, *Collier's* Collection.

46. Haycox to Chenery, 16 August 1939, *Collier's* Collection.

47. Haycox to Everitt, 23 January 1941; Everitt to Haycox, 30 January 1941; and Haycox to Everitt, 5 February 1941, Little, Brown Archives.

Chapter Five

1. "Virgins, Villains, and Varmints," in *The Western: A Collection of Critical Essays,* ed. James K. Folsom (Englewood Cliffs, N.J.: Prentice-Hall, 1979), 34.

2. Haycox to Ted Shane, 22 October 1948, Haycox Family Papers. The story appeared in *Collier's,* 20 November 1948.

3. "Cry Deep, Cry Still," *Collier's,* 20 November 1948; "Call This Land Home," *Saturday Evening Post,* 4 December 1948; and "Violent Interlude," *Saturday Evening Post,* 26 February 1949.

4. Haycox to Cameron, 29 April 1948, Little, Brown Archives.

5. Haycox to Cameron, 13 July 1949, Little, Brown Archives.

6. Richard S. Wheeler makes this point in "Grace under Pressure: A Beleaguered Literary Genre," *Roundup Quarterly* 5 (Winter 1992): 17–21, and "Writing Offbeat Western," *Chronicles,* August 1991, 20–23. Wheeler is one of the finest recent novelists to treat the West. Like Haycox, he has diverged from cowboy formulas to write historical novels that reveal the rich breadth of the frontier experience, including the important role played by women. See, for example, *Cashbox* (New York: Forge, 1994).

7. Haycox to Thacher, 31 July 1944, Haycox Collection.

8. Haycox to John A. Ford, 12 February 1948, Haycox Family Papers.

9. Haycox to Everitt, 24 May 1940, Little, Brown Archives.

10. "Phaethon on Gunsmoke Trail," 13.

11. Haycox to Thacher [1945–46], Haycox Collection.

12. "Writers: Dealers in Emotion," 250.

13. Haycox to Philip Souers, 13 November 1946, Haycox Collection.

14. Jill Marie Haycox, introduction to *Canyon Passage* (Boston: Gregg Press, 1979).

15. Haycox to Thacher, 16 May 1946, Haycox Collection.

16. Little, Brown to George Giguere, 13 September 1944 and 19 September 1944, Little, Brown Archives.

17. Haycox to Thacher, 31 July 1944, Haycox Collection.

18. Haycox to Thacher [December 1945], Haycox Collection.

19. Haycox to Thacher, two letters undated [1945], Haycox Collection.

20. Haycox to Thacher [late 1944], Haycox Collection.

21. Haycox to Thacher, 17 January 1945 and undated [1945], and Haycox to Sanders, 3 July 1947, Haycox Family Papers.

22. Haycox to Thacher [1945], Haycox Collection.

23. "No Escalator to Heaven," *Rotarian* 75 (October 1949): 6.

24. Sanders to Everitt, 16 October 1945, and Everitt to Sanders, 5 November 1945, Little, Brown Archives.

25. Haycox to Everitt, 7 March 1946 and 4 September 1946, Little, Brown Archives.

26. Haycox to Thacher, 16 May 1946, Haycox Collection.

27. Haycox to Cameron, 29 November 1949, Little, Brown Archives.

28. Haycox to Thacher, 16 May 1946, 15 August 1946, and 14 February 1947, Haycox Collection.

29. In a 29 July 1949 letter to Oswald West, Haycox wrote, "If I live long enough I plan to write about eight books on Oregon, each book covering a certain period of the history of the state" (Oregon Historical Society Library). West had been governor from 1910 to 1916, and Haycox wanted to pump him for material for one of those novels.

30. Haycox to Sanders, 19 March 1947, 18 June 1947, and 26 June 1947, Haycox Family Papers.

31. Haycox to Cameron, 31 July 1947, Little, Brown Archives.

32. Haycox to Cameron, 21 February 1949, Little, Brown Archives.

33. Haycox to Cameron, 11 April 1949, Little, Brown Archives.

34. Haycox to Cameron, 3 January 1950, Little, Brown Archives.

35. Haycox to Cameron, 5 May 1949, Little, Brown Archives.

36. Haycox to Thacher, undated [1949], Haycox Collection.

37. Lawrence Polliger to Little, Brown, 20 March 1952; Geral Chapman to Charles B. Blanchard, 9 May 1952, Little, Brown Archives.

38. Haycox to Cameron, 26 February 1950, Little, Brown Archives.

39. Cameron to Jill Haycox, 23 January 1951; Jill Haycox to Cameron, 26 January 1951, Little, Brown Archives.

40. Haycox to Cameron, 3 January 1950, Little, Brown Archives.

41. *Dear W. F. G.* (Boston: Little, Brown, 1952), 2; Cameron to Thacher, 8 January 1951, Little, Brown Archives.

42. Haycox to Cameron, 26 February and 6 March 1950, Little, Brown Archives.

Conclusion

1. *Western and Hard-Boiled Detective Fiction in America,* 3.

2. *West of Everything: The Inner Life of Westerns* (New York: Oxford

University Press, 1992), 7, 45.

3.   "Down These Streets a Mean Man Must Go," in *Self-Portrait*, 8–9.

4.   Joseph Conrad, *Chance* (Garden City, N.Y.: Doubleday, Page & Co., 1914), 302.

5.   "Fiction as Food," in *The Spice of Life* (Beaconsfield, England: Darwen Finlayson, 1964), 35–36.

6.   Haycox to Thacher, 21 July 1939, Haycox Collection.

7.   Leo Baker, "Nearing the Beginning," in *C. S. Lewis at the Breakfast Table*, ed. James T. Como (New York: Macmillan, 1979), 10.

8.   Diana Trilling, *The Beginning of the Journey* (New York: Harcourt Brace, 1993), 400.

9.   I have borrowed these words from Don D. Walker's description of what literary criticism of the western might concern itself with in "Essays in the Criticism of Western Literary Criticism, III: On De-mythologizing the Western," *The Possible Sack* 2 (August 1971): 3.

Selected Bibliography

PRIMARY WORKS

Novels

Action by Night. Boston: Little, Brown, 1943.
The Adventurers. Boston: Little, Brown, 1955.
Alder Gulch. Boston: Little, Brown, 1942.
The Border Trumpet. Boston: Little, Brown, 1939.
Bugles in the Afternoon. Boston: Little, Brown, 1944.
Canyon Passage. Boston: Little, Brown, 1945.
Chaffee of Roaring Horse. Garden City, N.Y.: Doubleday, Doran, 1930.
Dead Man Range. New York: Popular Library, 1957.
Deep West. Boston: Little, Brown, 1937.
The Earthbreakers. Boston: Little, Brown, 1952.
Free Grass. Garden City, N.Y.: Doubleday, Doran, 1929.
The Feudists. New York: Signet, 1960.
Head of the Mountain. New York: Popular Library, 1952.
Long Storm. Boston: Little, Brown, 1946.
Man in the Saddle. Boston: Little, Brown, 1938.
On the Prod. New York: Popular Library, 1957.
Return of a Fighter. New York: Dell, 1951.
A Rider of the High Mesa. New York: Popular Library, 1956.
Riders West. Garden City, N.Y.: Doubleday, Doran, 1934.
Rim of the Desert. Boston: Little, Brown, 1941.
Rough Air. Garden City, N.Y.: Doubleday, Doran, 1934.
Saddle and Ride. Boston: Little, Brown, 1940.
The Silver Desert. Garden City, N.Y.: Doubleday, Doran, 1935.
Starlight Rider. Garden City, N.Y.: Doubleday, Doran, 1935.
Sundown Jim. Boston: Little, Brown, 1938.
Trail Smoke. Garden City, N.Y.: Doubleday, Doran, 1936.
Trail Town. Boston: Little, Brown, 1941.
Trouble Shooter. Garden City, N.Y.: Doubleday, Doran, 1937.
Whispering Range. Garden City, N.Y.: Doubleday, Doran, 1931.
The Wild Bunch. Boston: Little, Brown, 1943.

Story Collections

Best Western Stories of Ernest Haycox. New York: Bantam, 1960.
Brand Fires on the Ridge. New York: Monarch Books, 1959.

By Rope and Lead. Boston: Little, Brown, 1951.
The Grim Canyon. New York: Popular Library, 1953.
Gun Talk. New York: Popular Library, 1953.
Guns of the Tom Dee. New York: Popular Giant Eagle Books, 1959.
Guns Up. New York: Popular Library, 1954.
The Last Rodeo. Boston: Little, Brown, 1956.
Lone Rider. New York: Popular Library, 1959.
Murder on the Frontier. Boston: Little, Brown, 1953.
Outlaw. Boston: Little, Brown, 1953.
Outlaw Guns. New York: Pyramid, 1964.
Pioneer Loves. Boston: Little, Brown, 1952.
Powder Smoke and Other Stories. New York: Avon, 1966.
Prairie Guns. Boston: Little, Brown, 1954.
Rawhide Range. New York: Popular Library, 1952.
Rough Justice. Boston: Little, Brown, 1952.
Secret River. New York: Popular Library, 1955.
Sixgun Duo. New York: Ace Books, 1965.
Trigger Trio. New York: Ace Books, 1966.
Vengeance Trail. New York: Popular Library, 1955.
Winds of Rebellion: Tales of the American Revolution. New York: Criterion, 1954.

Essays

"The Course of the Blue Eagle." *Rotarian*, December 1933, 6–8, 56–58.
"Is There a Northwest?" In *Northwest Harvest*, edited by V. L. O. Chittick,
    39–51. New York: Macmillan, 1948.
"Monsters over the Hill." *Rotarian*, December 1946, 7.
"No Escalator to Heaven." *Rotarian*, October 1949, 6.
"Peace Is What We Make It." *Rotarian*, November 1945, 7, 48–50.
"A Persistent Writer's Success." *Writer*, September 1922, 129–30.
"Sir Walter Excepting . . ." *Writer's Digest*, February 1942, 11–15.
"Writers: Dealers in Emotion." *Library Journal*, 15 February 1946, 248–51.

SECONDARY WORKS

Bibliography

Haycox, Jill, and John Chord. "Ernest Haycox Fiction—a Checklist." *Call
    Number* 25 (Fall 1963–Spring 1964): 4–27.

Articles and Parts of Books

Bold, Christine. "Ernest Haycox." In *Selling the Wild West: Popular Western
    Fiction, 1800 to 1960*, 104–23. Bloomington: University of Indiana Press,
    1987. Describes Haycox's vacillating development from pulp fiction to
    novels, showing how the markets shaped a fiction that progressed from
    formula to naturalism.

Easterwood, Thomas J. "The Ernest Haycox Memorial Library." *Call Number* 25
    (Fall 1963–Spring 1964): 31. Brief description of Haycox's personal
    library now housed in a designated room of the University of Oregon
    Library.
Etulain, Richard W. "Ernest Haycox: The Historical Western, 1937–43." *South
    Dakota Review* 5 (Spring 1967): 35–54. Informative exposition of the
    mid-career fiction.
————. "Ernest Haycox: Popular Novelist of the Pacific Northwest." In
    Northwest Perspectives: Essays on the Culture of the Pacific Northwest, edited by
    Edwin R. Bingham and Glen A. Love, 136–50. Seattle: University of
    Washington Press, 1979. Summarizes Haycox's career with emphasis on
    Bugles in the Afternoon and *The Earthbreakers.*
Fargo, James. "The Western and Ernest Haycox." *Prairie Schooner* 26 (1952):
    177–85. Appreciative summary of the fiction and an account of a visit
    with Haycox in 1945.
Gale, Robert L. "Ernest Haycox." In *Fifty Western Writers: A Bio-Bibliographical
    Sourcebook,* edited by Fred Erisman and Richard W. Etulain, 183–93.
    Westport, Conn.: Greenwood Press, 1982. Brief but informative treat-
    ment of biography, major themes, and critical response, with a bibliogra-
    phy.
Garfield, Brian. "Ernest Haycox: A Study in Style." *Roundup* 21 (February
    1973): 1–3, 5. Perceptive analysis of Haycox's use of language.
Haycox, Ernest, Jr. Introduction to *Bugles in the Afternoon.* Boston: Gregg Press,
    1978. Describes his father's writing methods and his insistence on histor-
    ical accuracy.
Haycox, Jill Marie. Introduction to *The Earthbreakers.* Boston: Gregg Press,
    1979. Random information about Haycox and and his literary estate.
————. "The Light of Other Days." *Roundup* 21 (October 1973): 1–2, 4–6.
    Describes her husband and the process of managing the literary estate
    after his death.
————. Introduction to *Canyon Passage.* Boston: Gregg Press, 1979. Describes
    the people and events of the Portland premiere of the film *Canyon Passage.*
Nesbitt, John D. "A New Look at Two Popular Western Classics." *South Dakota
    Review* 18 (Spring 1980): 30–42. Literary analysis of *Bugles in the
    Afternoon.*
DeVoto, Bernard. "Phaethon on Gunsmoke Trail." *Harper's,* December 1954,
    10–11, 14, 16. Argues that making serious fiction out of the western
    myth is impossible, but Haycox succeeded better than others in the
    attempt.

Dissertation

Etulain, Richard W. "The Literary Career of a Western Writer: Ernest Haycox,
    1899–1950." Ph.D. dissertation, University of Oregon, 1966. Thoroughly
    researched biographical-critical study.

Index

The Author

Stephen L. Tanner was educated at the University of Utah and the University of Wisconsin. He has taught at the University of Idaho and, as a Fulbright lecturer, in Brazil and Portugal. He is currently Ralph A. Britsch Humanities Professor of English at Brigham Young University, where he teaches American literature and literary criticism. He is the author of *Ken Kesey, Paul Elmer More: Literary Criticism as the History of Ideas*, and *Lionel Trilling*.

The Editor

Joseph M. Flora earned his B.A. (1956), M.A. (1957), and Ph.D. (1962) in English at the University of Michigan. In 1962 he joined the faculty of the University of North Carolina, where he is professor of English. His study *Hemingway's Nick Adams* (1984) won the Mayflower Award. He is also author of *Vardis Fisher* (1962), *William Ernest Henley* (1970), *Frederick Manfred* (1974), and *Ernest Hemingway: A Study of the Short Fiction* (1989). He is editor of *The English Short Story* (1985) and coeditor of *Southern Writers: A Biographical Dictionary* (1970), *Fifty Southern Writers before 1900* (1987), and *Fifty Southern Writers after 1900* (1987). He serves on the editorial boards of *Studies in Short Fiction* and *Southern Literary Journal*.